AN INTRODUCTION TO WILDLIFE REHABILITATION

AN INTRODUCTION TO

WILDLIFE REHABILITATION

By

Nancy A. Schwartz
Wildlife Rehabilitator

Copyright © 2007 by Nancy A. Schwartz.

ISBN:		Softcover		978-1-4257-3844-0

All rights reserved. No part of this book may be reproduced or transmitted in any form or by any means, electronic or mechanical, including photocopying, recording, or by any information storage and retrieval system, without permission in writing from the copyright owner.

This book was printed in the United States of America.

To order additional copies of this book, contact:
Xlibris Corporation
1-888-795-4274
www.Xlibris.com
Orders@Xlibris.com
36710

CONTENTS

Introduction 9

Supplies to Have On Hand 11

Zoonoses (diseases transmitted to humans) 13

    Bacterial 13
    Mycotic 16
    Viral 17
    Parasitic 19
    Protozoal 20
    Tick Borne 21

Does This Animal Really Need Help? 22

Questions & Answers 24

Wildlife Myths 27

Stages of Development 29

Orphan Mammal General Care 32

Orphan Ducklings/Goslings General Care 36

Orphan Songbird General Care 38

Dove and Pigeon Feeding Basics 43

Common Feeding Problems 45

Species Information—Mammal
- White-Tailed Deer 49
- Opossum 51
- Raccoon 53
- Eastern Cottontail Rabbit 55
- Gray Squirrel 56
- Woodchuck 58
- Red Fox 59
- Coyote 60
- Brown Bat 62
- Striped Skunk 64
- Thirteen-Lined Ground Squirrel 66

Species Information—Avian
- Great Egret 71
- Great Blue Heron 72
- Snowy Egret 73
- Herring Gull 74
- Mallard Duck 75
- Canada Goose 76
- Barn Owl 77
- Short-Eared Owl 78
- Long-Eared Owl 79
- Red-Tailed Hawk 80
- American Kestrel 81
- Peregrine Falcon 82
- Mourning Dove 84
- Pigeon 86
- Robin 88
- American Crow 90
- House Sparrow 92
- Starling 94

Basic Housing Requirements for Animals/Avians 96

Home-Made Incubator 99

Personal Safety 101

Rescue and Handling 103

Physical Exam 105

Wildlife Admission Form 108

Initial Mammal Exam Form 109

Initial Avian Exam Form 110

First-Aid Avian Basics 111

Treatment and Release of Oiled Birds 114

Vacination Protocols 116

Preparing For Release 118

Diseases Common in Species 120
    Opossum 120
    Raccoon 121
    Red Fox 123
    Gray Squirrel 123
    Fox Squirrel 123
    Water Birds 124
    Dove and Pigeon 124
    All Birds 126

Commonly Used Conversion Factors 128

Permit Overview 130

INTRODUCTION

Wildlife rehabilitation is the temporary care of injured or orphaned native wildlife, so that they may be released back into their native habitat. While there are a growing number of wildlife rehabilitation centers across North America, the majority of wildlife rehabilitators operate out of home-based rehabilitation facilities. They use areas of their homes and yards that are isolated from other family activities. Wildlife rehabilitators must perform a variety of duties. They spend considerable time talking with the public on the phone to prevent human-wildlife conflicts, resolve any problems that have already occurred, and arrange for the public to surrender wild animals that need care.

Every year, tens of thousands of baby wild animals are rescued that didn't need to be rescued. In most cases, well meaning people are trying to help an animal that they believe has been abandoned by its parents. All wild animals have very strong parental instincts and will often risk their own lives in defense of their young. It would be extremely rare for a wild animal to abandon its young. Many wild infants are believed to be orphaned because a parent animal is not seen. Some mammals, such as rabbits and deer keep a distance from their young during the day so as not to draw attention to their location. Steps should be taken to determine if the young are being attended by a parent before any human intervention is instituted.

This book was designed to help those who are interested in learning more about wildlife and their rehabilitation needs. The author, authorities by experience, and has saved thousands of animals and birds over the years tending wildlife. Keep in mind, anyone interested in wildlife rehabilitation needs to have wildlife permit(s) issued by the state in order to do so. If you do not qualify for a permit, you will still be able to learn and work under the direct supervision of a wildlife rehabilitator who carries the proper permits. Depending on the species of animal or bird you are interested in rehabilitating you may need permits issued by U.S. Fish & Wildlife as well. Contact your local Department of Natural Resources for more information.

I hope you find the contents of this book to be of value to you in your search for learning more about our wildlife. Good luck and thanks to all who have dedicated their time in saving our wildlife.

SUPPLIES TO HAVE ON HAND

Basic Food List

Esbilac Powder (not liquid)
KMR Powder (not liquid)
Baby rice cereal
Applesauce (natural)
Chicken scratch/starter non-medicated
Flock raiser/duck starter
Cracked corn
Dry puppy/dog chow
Dry cat/kitten chow
Canned cat food (fish or chicken flavors)
Rodent chow
Wild bird seed, sunflower seeds, dove food
Rabbit pellets, timothy hay
Frozen mice or beef heart strips
Frozen mixed vegetables and frozen mixed fruit
Cheerios cereal
Canned freeze-dried mealworms and crickets

General Supply List

Caging appropriate for specific species
Gram scale
Heating pads or hot water bottles
Bandage scissors
Tweezers

Towels
Latex gloves
Heavy leather gloves (welder's gloves)
Luer tip syringes for feeding
Pet nursers (different sizes)
Margarine tubs or cardboard boxes for nests
Eye wash (saline flush)
Chlorhexidine solution
Bandage Kit—gauze, non-adhesive pads, vet-wrap, and porous tape
Probiacin or Bene-Bac
Triple antibiotic cream
Flea powder
Pedialyte
Nutrical (vitamin supplement)
Dawn dishwashing liquid

ZOONOSES

Zoonoses is a disease which can be transmitted from animals to humans under natural conditions. If you use standard precautions, excellent hygiene, and good ventilation in your work area, you will eliminate risks from most zoonotic diseases. Always wear latex gloves when handling wildlife. Check with your state fish and game agency to determine what diseases are prevalent in your area.

Bacterial Diseases

These diseases can be transmitted by contamination through broken skin of wounds or abrasions, contamination of the mucous membranes with urine or feces, and sometimes through bruised skin.

Brucellosis

- **Hosts**
  White tailed deer, raccoon, fox, and coyote
- **Transmission**
  By contact with blood, urine, feces, vaginal discharge, and tissues or fetuses of infected animals.
- **Symptoms**
  The animal may appear to have septicemia. The source of infection may be from the lymph nodes, spleen, reproductive organs, or joints.

Psittacosis

- **Hosts**
  Birds including pigeons, raptors, and finches
- **Transmission**
  The bacteria are contained in the tissues, droppings, and nasal discharges of infected birds. The most common route of infection to humans is through fecal-oral contamination and inhalation of dried droppings and discharge.
- **Symptoms**
  Signs in animals may include respiratory distress, conjunctivitis, green diarrhea tinged with blood, and emaciation due to decreased appetite.

Salmonellas

- **Hosts**
  Birds, reptiles, and mammals
- **Transmission**
  Through fecal contamination, usually fecal-oral contamination. The bacteria may contaminate food, water, or live on surfaces not properly cleaned.
- **Symptoms**
  In animals the symptoms are not as obvious. When symptoms are present, they may include weakness, drowsiness, depression, convulsions, trembling, gasping of air, vomiting, diarrhea, and a slight fever. The shedding period of these bacteria lasts for some time following infection. Some animals can become carriers.

Leptospirosis

- **Hosts**
  Raccoon, skunk, opossum, rodents, and other mammals
- **Transmission**
  Contact with infected food, water, soil and especially urine or direct contact with an infected animal. This disease can be transmitted by contact with open wounds, abrasions, or intact skin.
- **Symptoms**
  Symptoms are usually not as apparent in wild animals. Animals may suffer acute renal failure, dehydration, vomiting, fever, increased thirst, be reluctant to move, and appear jaundice.

Tularemia

- **Hosts**
  Rabbits and rodents
- **Transmission**
  Handling infected animals, inhalation of bacteria, and contamination of cuts, mosquito, tick or fly bites.
- **Symptoms**
  Animals appear to have a fever, lymphadenopathy, draining abscesses, and fatal bacteremia.

Mycotic Diseases—Fungi often found in the environment cause these diseases.

Aspergillosis

- **Hosts**
  Birds, especially raptors and waterfowl
- **Transmission**
  Infected birds shed spores of the disease that may be inhaled by humans.
- **Symptoms**
  Birds exhibit respiratory symptoms. Affected birds may be emaciated and have problems breathing.

Histoplasmosis

- **Hosts**
  Birds and bats
- **Transmission**
  Spread through the inhalation of infective spores. The organisms are present in the soil and may grow in soil that contains decayed bat or bird droppings. This mainly occurs around roost areas that have been established for at least three years.
- **Symptoms**
  Will present as a mild upper respiratory infection, with a chronic persistent cough, and weight loss.

Viral Disease—Rabies

Any wild mammal that you come into contact with should be considered potential carriers and precaution must be taken. When handling a baby raccoon or even a wild kitten it is easy to forget that age has no bearing on whether or not the animal is carrying the rabies virus. To be safe, use standard precautions, and handle all mammals as though they may be possibly carrying this virus.

- **Hosts**
  Any warm blooded mammal
- **Transmission**
  The virus is transmitted in the saliva of the host animal and may enter the body by introduction of saliva into cuts and open wounds or contact with mucus membranes.
- **Symptoms**
  Signs can include restlessness, aggression, unusual friendliness, salivation, ataxia, paralysis, and convulsions.

Rabies is one of the best known of all the viruses. Rabies is an infectious viral disease that affects the nervous system of humans and other warm-blooded animals. Understanding the most common routes of exposure and what presents a risk is necessary to determine whether or not human post-exposure prophylaxis is needed.

- Bite
- Contamination of Open Wounds
- Oral Exposure
- Inhalation
- Ocular Exposure
- Non-bite exposures include inhalation of aerosol and corneal and organ transplantation.

Wild Animal Exposure

With wild carnivores, if the source of exposure is obvious such as a bite or gross contamination of eyes, nose, or mouth with material from the animal, it's considered high risk. If the animal is available, testing to get a definitive diagnosis will determine post-exposure needs. If the animal is not available, post-exposure is usually needed.

For livestock and small mammals such as rabbits, hamsters, and guinea pigs, these generally present low-risk situations. The decision can be made on a case-by-case basis, often in consultation with local and state health officials. Rodents are not a reservoir for rabies. Naturally infected cases are extremely rare. Scenarios leading to infection of domestic rodents are rabbits housed in outdoor hutches, often with a known history of a wound, or the observation of a suspect rabies reservoir rabies species such as a skunk or a raccoon in the vicinity.

Large bodied wild rodents, such as woodchucks (ground hogs) or beavers have been positive for rabies in areas with the raccoon rabies virus variant. They may survive an attack by a rabid raccoon and go on to develop rabies. Potential exposure situations with smaller rodents, such as chipmunks, squirrels, wild mice, pet hamsters and gerbils, overwhelmingly do not require post-exposure. For unknown reasons, it is rare for an opossum to be a rabies carrier. Rabies in bats is widespread geographically throughout the United States.

Parasitic Diseases

Roundworm

These are the ascarids that relate to specific hosts. Toxocara canis, Toxocara cati and Toxacsaris Leonia are the most common parasites of dogs, cats, and foxes. Baylisascaris columnaris are commonly found in raccoons.

Baylisascaris Procyonis

- **Hosts**
  Raccoons
- **Transmission**
  Through fecal-oral ingestion of the roundworm eggs.
- **Symptoms**
  Often in adult raccoons there is no sign of the infection. Young raccoons may have diarrhea, general malaise, and fussiness. Roundworms may show in the feces. In other animals, irreversible central nervous damage and possible death may occur.

Sarcoptic Mange

- **Hosts**
  Coyote, fox, other mammals
- **Transmission**
  This mite transfers by direct contact during handling.
- **Symptoms**
  Typically red, crusty lesions appear on the ears, elbows, and elsewhere on the trunk of the animal. Intense itching is seen and fur loss. Secondary bacterial skin infections may be present due to self-trauma.

Protozoal Diseases

Giardiasis

- **Hosts**
  Beaver, muskrat, waterfowl
- **Transmission**
  Ingestion of water contaminated with infected feces or oral ingestion of contaminated feces.
- **Symptoms**
  A variety of intestinal infections may be seen including chronic diarrhea, abdominal cramps, bloating, weight loss, and frequent pale stools.

Tick Borne Diseases

Lyme Disease

Lyme disease is currently the most common tick-borne disease.

- **Hosts**
  Deer ticks
- **Transmission**
  The bite of infected ticks.
- **Symptoms**
  Lameness is the most common sign seen in animals. Other signs include fever, anorexia, nephritis, and cardiac abnormalities.

Ehrlichiosis

- **Hosts**
  Deer ticks
- **Transmission**
  The bite of infected ticks.
- **Symptoms**
  Symptoms in animals include weakness, cough, labored breathing, intermittent fever, arthritis, discharge from nose or eye, increased thirst or urination, anorexia, seizures, nose bleeds, and swelling of the legs or lymph nodes.

DOES THIS ANIMAL REALLY NEED HELP?

- Be certain the animal is injured or orphaned, watch and wait before taking any action.

- With species such as deer and rabbits, the mother may be nearby.

- If it is a feathered young bird hopping on the ground, watch to see if the parent birds are nearby in a tree watching their fledgling.

- If a bird has fallen out of a nest and you can get to the nest, pick up the bird carefully and put it in the nest.

- If a bird hits a window, check it for signs of injury such as bleeding, head tilt, broken wing, etc. If it appears to be only stunned, put it in a box and wait two to three hours; at the end of that time see if it will fly away.

- Some plovers and killdeer, while running away from you, perform the customary broken wing act. This action is designed to focus a predator's attention on the mother and away from the chicks.

- Coyotes, dogs, cats, raccoons, construction, etc. are not reasons for baby animals to be removed. These are things that they must encounter on a daily basis. The mother will move her young away from danger when she is able. Try not to interfere with their natural habits and behavior.

If you find baby bunnies:

If their nest has been damaged, it can be repaired. Look for a shallow depression lined with grass or fur. Place the babies in the nest with a light layer of grass to hide them. Leave the area or the mother will not return. She will only feed her young once every 24 hours. When she has finished nursing, she will maintain a safe distance from her nest in hopes of keeping predators away.

If you find healthy bunnies that are four to five inches long, able to hop, with eyes open and ears up, they do not need help. They can survive on their own.

If you find a fawn:

Mothers normally leave their babies to feed. Often does will not return to their fawns until well after dark.

Keep yourself and pets far away from the fawn. It may take a good 24 hours for a doe to feel safe enough to return to her fawn. If a mother were to return prematurely, she might risk leading a predator directly to her fawn.

Do not touch the fawn! For the first five days after birth, fawns will not run when approached. Instead they will exhibit "freeze behavior". From the seventh day on, fawns will exhibit "flight behavior" when approached. By one month of age, fawns venture out to browse with their mothers.

QUESTIONS & ANSWERS

My dog found baby bunnies in the yard, what should I do?

Place the bunnies back where you found them. If they are still in a nest, place a 2' x 2' or larger piece of flat wood over the nest, with the wood perched on bricks or other material so that the parent cottontail can get to the youngsters but dogs or cats can't. Until the bunnies have left the nest, which may be around two to three weeks, keep your dog on a leash so it does not bother the nest of bunnies.

I found a baby squirrel, what should I do?

Put the squirrel in a small box at the base of the tree near where you found it, the parent squirrel will retrieve the baby if it is left alone. If she does not return by dark, provide warmth until it can be transferred to a wildlife rehabilitator.

A baby bird has fallen from its nest in a tree in my backyard, should I bring it into the house and feed it until it is able to fly?

No. The best thing to do is put the bird carefully back into the nest, or place it into some thick shrubbery or other protected space in your yard, the parents will continue to feed and care for the fledgling. Keep your pet(s) in the house to allow the young bird's parent to care for it. As a last resort, a nestling can be placed in a clear plastic butter dish with a napkin in the bottom. This artificial nest can then be put in a bush or tree near the place the nestling was found.

When walking through the woods I saw several baby raccoons on the ground near a large tree with no adult in sight, should I bring them home and care for them?

No. Most likely the young raccoons are merely exploring, and their mother is nearby. They are probably old enough to be fully capable of climbing back up the tree to their den when they are ready to return and if they were too young to climb their mother would carry them back.

A bird flew into my window and seems unable to fly, what should I do?

Most likely the bird is just stunned from the impact. Wait a few minutes, generally they recover and fly off. Keep your pets in the house and leave the bird alone so that it has a chance to recover on its own. If necessary, place the bird in a box and keep it in a quiet, dark area for a couple hours, then release it.

There is this bird banging itself into our window. Why is he doing this and how can I get him to stop?

This bird may be protecting its territory because it sees its own reflection and thinks it is another male bird invading his turf. You can tape streamers or balloons to the outside of the window to deter the bird, or cover the most common areas of the window with newspaper to block the glare on the window.

There is a bird in my yard and it can not fly.

If the bird is active, chirping, and hopping around it is probably a fledgling or juvenile bird too big to remain in the nest and within a week it will fly away. The parent birds are most likely close by, finding it with their communicative chirps and feeding it.

If the bird is not active, eyes closed, not chirping or hopping, feather-less or any one of these, contact a wildlife rehabilitator. Some babies accidentally fall from the nest. If there are apparent injuries, transfer to a rehabilitator. If it is possible to return it to the nest, please do so in a safe cautionary fashion. Do not attempt this with possible injury to yourself.

If the bird is an adult and not flying, contact a wildlife rehabilitator for transfer and further instructions.

There are workers replacing gutters on my home. They found a nest in it, what should be done with it?

The entire nest and contents of any eggs or young can be placed in a small box and placed as close as possible to the original nest site, keep in mind it needs to be raised off the ground to prevent predation. The mother will continue to care for her babies.

I saw a (hawk, owl, heron, goose) that acts like it has a broken wing, what should I do?

Since there are federal laws against possession of migratory birds, including raptors and water birds, contact a rehabilitator that has the correct permits and follow their instructions. *Do not attempt to feed these birds*, giving them the wrong food may complicate their recovery or even cause their demise.

Keep in mind that death is an integral part of the natural world. It may even represent life to another wildlife species which can use that animal as sustenance or to feed their young. While it may seem disheartening to see a young animal die, it represents only one individual in an entire population which could not thrive if all young born survived.

WILDLIFE MYTHS

If you touch a baby bird or baby bunny, the mother will reject or kill it.

Mothers will not reject their young, many baby wild animals have no body odor and predators cannot smell them. If you handle a wild baby you will place your scent on it and a predator may detect it, get curious, find the baby and eat it.

I found a baby rabbit and the mother has not come back.

Mom usually only feeds once during the night and only for a short period of time; this is to keep potential predators away. Keep in mind she built the nest, delivered the litter and has been caring for them without being observed. She will continue to do so. If you are not sure, take a piece of yarn and make an "X" over the nest before the evening. Check the nest the next morning to see if it has been moved.

If you see a night predator out during the daytime, it is rabid.

Not always. If a mother has babies in the den she may be hunting. Animals may also be routed from their den accidentally. You should never approach any wildlife though, especially if its behavior is uncharacteristic.

People hand-rearing wildlife is an acceptable alternative to parent rearing.

Human intervention should be the absolute last resort for any wild infant. While hand-rearing may facilitate the immediate survival of an infant animal, it greatly reduces its potential for long term survival in the wild. Hand-reared animals do not have the same survival skills, and perhaps more importantly, may not have the fear instincts of a parent-reared animal.

If a wild animal is imprinted or socialized, it might make a good pet.

While they may appear cute and cuddly, when they grow up they will have natural urges that will make them unsuitable as pets. Even the "tamest" animal is unpredictable and can attack you. If an imprinted animal escapes, it may succumb to a horrible ending due to the lack of fear from humans and predators. Wild animals also harbor disease and parasites that can be transmitted to humans and domestic animals.

STAGES OF DEVELOPMENT

Squirrel

Birth to 1 week	3-4 inches long; pink, no fur, eyes closed
1 to 2 weeks	Pink, scant fur, eyes closed
2 to 3 weeks	4-5 inches long; scant fur, eyes closed
3 to 4 weeks	5-6 inches long; fur all over, eyes opening at the corners
4 to 5 weeks	6-7 inches long; eyes open, cannot curl tail
5 to 6 weeks	Can curl their tail; appearance of upper incisors
6 to 7 weeks	7-8 inches long; fully furred including underside of the tail, can sit up
8 to 12 weeks	Long fur, bushy tail, increasingly active

Chipmunk

Birth to 1 week	1.5 to 2 inches long; no fur, eyes closed
1 to 2 weeks	Stripes appear, eyes closed, becoming active
2 to 3 weeks	Color pattern fully developed, eyes closed, looks like a miniature adult
3 to 4 weeks	Eyes and ears are open
4 to 5 weeks	Increasingly active
7 to 8 weeks	Thick coat and very active

Woodchuck

Birth	About 4 inches long; eyes closed, no fur, skin wrinkled
1 week	Eyes closed, skin becomes pigmented
2 weeks	Eyes closed, inactive, fur starting to come in over body
3 weeks	Eyes closed, fully furred, beginning to crawl
4 weeks	Eyes first open, more active
6 weeks	Steady on feet

Skunk

Birth	Nearly naked, fine hair showing black and white pattern, eyes and ears are closed
1 week	Slightly furred, skin becoming pigmented
2 weeks	Fully furred, eyes still closed
3 weeks	Eyes and ears open
4 to 5 weeks	Becoming active, beginning to walk

Raccoon

Birth to 1 week	Eyes and ears are closed, face mask and tail rings barely visible, very little fur on the back and sides, no fur on the stomach
1 to 2 weeks	Eyelids have begun to separate slightly (thin slit), able to crawl (cannot support their weight), back and sides of infant's body are covered with fur
2 to 3 weeks	Facial skin fully furred, mask and tail rings more prominent as hair develops
3 to 4 weeks	Eyes begin to open, ears are open, respond to sights and sounds, developed characteristic vocalization, fully furred, tail rings apparent, can support their own weight
4 to 6 weeks	Eyes are open, well furred, canines and incisors visible, can walk, run, and climb
6 to 7 weeks	Good proficiency at walking, running, climbing, very active, sometimes rough fighting characterized by

	growling, squealing, wrestling and imitation of adult defense postures, molars can be felt
8 to 10 weeks	Becoming increasingly active

Opossum

Birth	Hairless pinkies, no larger than a dime, eyes closed
1 to 3 weeks	Eyes still closed, hairless
6 to 7 weeks	Eyes open, have hair, grasping with their hands and feet, becoming active, body (not including tail) is approximately three inches long
8 to 9 weeks	Leave the mother's pouch and are carried on her back

Cottontail Rabbit

Birth	Eyes closed, ears flat, hairless
1 week	Eyes begin to open and are fully furred, ears up
2 weeks	Eyes open, begins to explore outside of the nest
3 to 4 weeks	Weaned, very active, approximately four inches long

Jackrabbit

The jackrabbit is a hare, which means its young are born with fur and with their eyes open.

ORPHAN MAMMAL GENERAL CARE

It is *IMPERATIVE* that the baby's body core temperature be at an acceptable level *BEFORE* attempting to feed it. Trying to feed a cold orphan may result in death. Put the baby(s) in a plastic or cardboard box with soft material as a base. *NO* toweling material as the baby's toenails could snag causing harm. Place a heating pad, set on *LOW* underneath *HALF* the box and keep it in a warm, dark place until the baby is stabilized. If you do not have a heating pad, a water bottle filled with hot water and *TIGHTLY* capped will do. Once the baby(s) are stabilized, usually within several hours, offer a hydrating solution such as warmed Pedialyte or water *SLOWLY* with a syringe or an eye dropper and then again in a few hours.

WARNING: No matter how small they are, these babies will climb. Always cover any container housing young, punch holes in the top for air ventilation. Make a pocket in the middle of the nesting materiel used and place the baby(s) in the pocket, then lightly cover the baby(s) to keep them warm and the heat in.

Once the baby(s) are calm and accepting the hydrating solution, begin offering a puppy milk replacer powder formula (Esbilac) or the kitten milk replacer powder formula (KMR) for that species. *DO NOT* offer whole milk, wildlife cannot tolerate whole milk and this could cause a deadly digestive bacterial infection. A feeding schedule of every six to eight hours is sufficient. In young with *eyes that are still closed,* feed the milk replacer diluted with water only without the additives listed.

SQUIRREL & CHIPMUNK

Young, eyes open

2 parts pedialyte or water
1 part powdered Esbilac puppy milk replacer
1 part baby rice cereal
1 part applesauce (natural)

Adult

Rodent chow
Hamster diet
Sunflower seed
Cracked corn, nuts

OPOSSUM

Young, eyes open

2 parts pedialyte or water
1 part powdered Esbilac puppy milk replacer
1 part baby rice cereal
1 part applesauce (natural)

Adult

Vegetables, fruit 20%
Hard boiled egg, yogurt
Cat chow (not kitten)
Cooked chicken

RACCOON

Young, eyes open

2 parts pedialyte or water
1 part powdered KMR kitten milk replacer
1 part baby rice cereal
1 part applesauce (natural)

Adult

Dry cat food
Fruit
Vegetables
Cooked chicken

WOODCHUCK

Young, eyes open

2 parts pedialyte or water
1 part powdered Esbilac puppy milk replacer
1 part baby rice cereal
1 part applesauce (natural)

Adult

Prairie dog food
Rabbit pellets
Timothy hay

RABBIT

Young, eyes open   Adult

2 parts pedialyte or water   Kale and dandelion
1 part powdered KMR kitten milk replacer   Timothy hay
NO lettuce   Rabbit pellets

SKUNK

Young, eyes open   Adult

2 parts pedialyte or water   Nuts and fruits
1 part powdered Esbilac puppy milk replacer   Dry cat food
1 part baby rice cereal   Vegetables
1 part applesauce (natural)   Cooked meat

FAWN

                                                    Adult

Powdered Ewe replacement milk (mix accordingly)   Hay
1 teaspoon Karo Syrup   Dandelion leaves
½ cup baby mixed grain cereal   Goat mix
NO Alfalfa

- With baby wild animals, they may need assistance with urinating and defecating. Use warm water and a cotton ball to gently massage the genital area after every feeding.

- Keep in mind depending on the age of the young; they may require a minimum of three to four months of care before they can be released back into the wild.

- Minimum human contact is required to keep them from being used to people. Also they should not be exposed to dogs or cats since they are predators and a threat to the young when released back into the wild. The young need to know to flee when seeing us or other potential hazardous situations.

- Try to determine the animal's age and feed the age-appropriate diet. These diets are not by any means complete or meant to be used long-term. *These diets are strictly for emergency short-term use.*

ORPHAN DUCKLINGS OR GOSLINGS

Ducklings and goslings are precocial birds. They have the ability to walk and feed themselves.

Diet for ducklings and goslings

> Chicken scratch starter (non-medicated) or flock raiser for game birds fed daily

> Fresh greens such as dandelion, mustard greens, kale, chickweed, and an assortment of grasses fed daily

> Freeze dried insects such as mealworms or small crickets given a couple times a week

Do not put these birds in water to swim or place a water dish in their box while unattended. Downy waterfowl are protected by oil from their mother's oil gland. They do not have the ability to generate this oil on their own. If they are placed in water they cannot get out of, they will eventually become waterlogged and die. They may also become hypothermic and drown, even in shallow water.

Keep them warm by providing a source of heat. If they are placed in a box, keep the temperature at 80-85 degrees Fahrenheit by placing a heating pad set on low underneath the box. If they are kept in a small mammal cage you can provide warmth by using a reptile heatlamp placed at a comfortable distance to avoid overheating the young. Heat should be provided at one end of the cage so that the young can move out of the light if they get too hot.

Do not put any new bird(s) in with an established group of other birds, even of the same species. Newcomers, even if slightly larger, can be pecked to death.

Bread is a common misconception. Adult birds have gravel in their crop that allows bread to be broken down for digestion. Young babies do not have the benefit of gravel and, as a result, the bread will become compacted in their crop. This can cause death.

Goslings and ducklings should be fully feathered in approximately 45 days post hatching. At this point they should be moved to a flight pen. They should be placed in a safe enclosure that is large enough for them to exercise their wings and gain some flight experience. A pool area for them to bathe and swim in will also be needed. Remember, they need to be able to escape a predator when they are released back into the wild. The more strength and exercise they receive will help them maneuver obstacles in their path as well.

ORPHAN SONGBIRD GENERAL CARE

Baby bird(s) need extra heat until they are feathered. Build a nest from paper towels, toilet paper, or tissues. You can use a margarine tub, cereal type bowl, or dish to hold the nest together. The bottom of the nest where their feet rest should be scrunched so that they can grip it with their feet. The nest must be snug, since the bird's legs are made strong by pushing against the sides of the nest.

At each meal the baby bird(s) will lift their rear ends up over the edge of the nest and release a "fecal bubble" which is the stool. The nest should be cleaned after each feeding. Clean off the bird right away if any food or stool gets onto their skin or feathers. Listed are several examples of diets that are used for feedings.

MacLeod Passerine Diet

½ cup Purina ProPlan kitten (with just enough water to soften)
2 hard boiled egg whites
3 tablespoons Science Diet feline growth canned
2 tablespoons freeze dried insects (some flies a must)
½ tablespoon knox blox (gelatin once prepared)
800 mg Calcium (4 low sodium regular Tums work well)
100 mg Vitamin C

Robin Nestling Diet

Robins in the wild take in a variety of foods such as fruits, berries, insects, grains, earthworms, and insects such as beetle grubs, caterpillars, and grasshoppers. Robins are flexible and will turn to whichever food is most readily accessible.

The following rehabilitation diet is appropriate for feeding robins. This diet is good for any age nestling, but when feeding young less than five days old, more water should be added.

> 1 jar strained chicken baby food
> 1 cup adult cat food (quality brand)
> 1½ cups warm water
> ½ teaspoon bird vitamins
> ½ teaspoon brewer's yeast—not baking yeast

Put warm water in blender. Add dry cat food and soak for 30 minutes. Blend until smooth and add baby food, vitamins, and brewer's yeast. Blend together and store in refrigerator or freeze for future use.

Starling Nestling Diet

Starlings in the wild take in a variety of foods such as invertebrates, fruits and berries, insects, grains, and even animal feed or garbage.

> 1 cup of soaked dog/cat food
> ¼ cup applesauce (natural)
> 1 hard boiled egg
> Avian vitamins (use dosage on bottle)
> Calcium 750 mg (ground into powder and dissolve into a little water)

Mix all ingredients together with some warm water to make it into a paste. The formula can be divided into portions and frozen. Discard any unused portion kept at room temperature after an hour.

You can mix different foods in the formula such as mashed sweet potatoes or carrots. You may use jarred baby food such as peas or strained chicken as well.

When feeding, use something flat such as a popsicle stick or a straw with the end cut off to make a scoop. Do not use toothpicks, Q-tips or any other very small object for feeding.

Adult Bird Diet

> Poultry layer scratch (avoid poultry starter as it has medicine in it)
> Dry cat food (32% protein and 9% fat)
> Sweet potato cooked
> Carrots grated
> Dark green leafy vegetables

Supplements

> Feed a boiled or scrambled egg, boiled chicken, and any other types of protein foods two to three times a week.
>
> There are a variety of freeze dried insects readily available. You may offer mealworms, crickets, caterpillars, and grasshoppers.
>
> Remove any cooked foods after a couple of hours.

American Crow Nestling Diet

American crows are omnivores and will eat almost anything. They store food items such as meat and nuts in short-term hiding places in different areas. They may be covered with leaves or other material on the ground or hidden in tree crevices. During the breeding season they consume insects, worms, fruits, grains, and nuts. They prey on small animals such as frogs, mice, and young rabbits. They also scavenge on carrion such as roadkill. They are aggressive nest predators, preying on the eggs and nestlings of smaller songbirds. In the fall and winter they will eat more nuts and occasionally will eat from bird feeders.

The following rehabilitation diets are appropriate for feeding crows.

Avoid giving baby birds syringes of water, the water may go down their trachea and drown them. They will be able to absorb enough water with the diet provided below. Juvenile and adult birds should have water available at all times in a proper water bowl, you should never force a bird to drink water.

Baby Bird Food Recipe

- 1 cup dry puppy food (quality brand)
- 1 cup water
- 1 teaspoon bird vitamin powder
- 1 teaspoon calcium powder
- 1 shelled hard-boiled egg
- 1 4.5 ounce jar of banana baby food

Combine warm water and dry puppy food in a food processor and soak for 20 minutes. Blend until smooth and add the rest of the ingredients, blend together. Mix until it is a fine paste, add additional water if needed. You can store any excess in the freezer in small containers. Discard any unused thawed food at the end of the day.

Juvenile or Adult food Recipe

- 4 cups dry puppy food (quality brand)
- 2 cups water
- 1 teaspoon bird vitamin powder
- 1/2 hard-boiled egg
- 1/6 cup fruit such as apples, pears
- 1/6 cup green vegetable such as zucchini or cucumber
- 1/6 cup yellow or orange vegetable such as carrots, squash

Mix together dog food, water, and vitamins. Chop vegetables, fruit, and egg in a food processor. Mix all ingredients together and store in the refrigerator. Discard any unused food at the end of the day.

Supplements for Juvenile and Adult birds, use a variety sparingly and keep the diet balanced.

- Frozen chick that is thawed
- Frozen mouse that is thawed
- Hard-boiled egg with shell
- Freeze dried mealworms, crickets and other insects
- Veggie tidbits like frozen corn kernels
- Fruit chunks, berries
- Cooked sweet potato
- Dry cat food that has colored kibble
- Peanuts, unsalted, in the shell, cracked and out of the shell

Hatchlings

Hatchlings are totally bald or have just a few downy feathers. They may have trouble holding their heads upright. They need to be fed every 15 minutes regularly dawn to dusk. They grow so fast that missing a meal can create a weakness during their developmental phase at that time. "Hunger stripes" are weak stripes seen in the feathers of birds that have gone without food during the growth phase of the feathers. Hatchlings need to be kept at a temperature of 90-95 degrees.

Nestlings

Nestlings are beginning to get feathers, can hold their heads up and have control when grasping and reaching for food. Young nestlings must be fed every 30 minutes, nestlings that are trying to stand up need to be fed every hour. These babies need to be kept at a temperature of 85-90 degrees.

Fledglings

Fledglings will be standing and moving around in the nest area. They may be perching and even trying short flights. Fledglings can be maintained at room temperature, check them often at first to make sure they are adjusting well to the temperature. They should have food and water available. They need to be fed every hour until you are sure they are eating enough on their own.

DOVE AND PIGEON FEEDING BASICS

Dove and pigeons are fed a very different diet by their parents. The parents produce a cheesy-like substance which they regurgitate to their young. Doves and pigeons do not require the constant feeding needed by other commonly rescued nestlings. About six feedings a day is adequate for them. These birds store their food in their crops and swallow as necessary. When feeding, the crop should bulge slightly, but it should never become so loaded as to appear to stretch the skin. Reversely, the crop should never be allowed to become empty except at night.

Do not over-feed doves or pigeons. This can cause serious health problems. They will often ask for more food than they need, so it's up to you to figure out the appropriate amount they actually need. Start with smaller amounts of food and check their crops to see when they are empty. Adjust the amount of food as necessary.

When feeding doves or pigeons, it is a good idea to offer them water to drink, since unlike songbirds, they do sometimes require it. This should never be done forcibly, and a water dish should never be left in the box. Slide a very small cup filled with water toward the bird, and very gently dip the tip of the beak into the water so that the beak points in a vertical position. If the bird is thirsty, he will start drinking in this position. Take care not to accidentally splash water on him or around the nose, and do not dip the bird's beak into the water so that the nasal openings become wet. If the MacLeod Dove Formula is sufficiently moist, it is likely the bird will not need to drink until the finch seed is added. Once the bird is sufficiently mobile, provide a hanging water bin.

Getting the young of these species to eat can sometimes be difficult. As opposed to automatically opening their mouths when you present the food, young doves and pigeons must "fish out" food from their parents mouths. As a feeding signal, parents place their beaks over the beaks of their young, and "tap" a couple of times. Then the chick knows it is time to get to work.

MacLeod Dove Formula (for doves and pigeons)

> 1 jar strained beef baby food
> 1 tablespoon finely ground corn meal (yellow or white)
> 1 whole hard-boiled egg, finely chopped
> ¼ teaspoon wheat germ flakes
> ¼ teaspoon brewers yeast (for B-complex vitamins)
> ½ inch ribbon of Nutrical squeezed from tube

Mix with water until the mixture is a medium syrup consistency.

When the nestling is at least half feathered, add just a pinch of fine grit to formula.

When feathers are beginning to open (about 10 days old) the diet should consist of 80% MacLeod Dove Formula and 20% very small finch seed, mixed together.

COMMON FEEDING PROBLEMS

Inhalation of formula

When this occurs slow down or change to a smaller feeding tool. Keep in mind the young should be fed upright not lying on their backs, this will also help keep the young from aspirating formula.

Diarrhea

Diarrhea is most often caused by overfeeding. At the first sign of diarrhea, cut back the amount of formula given. If diarrhea persists, dilute the formula with Pedialyte, Lactated Ringers Solution or other re-hydrating solutions.

With severe cases of diarrhea, stop the formula altogether. Feed a re-hydrating solution for 12-24 hours and then slowly reintroduce the formula.

Bloat

Bloat may be caused by overfeeding, feeding the wrong formula, intestinal parasites, changes in diet, constipation or internal abnormalities. Once bloat is identified, stop feedings until it is resolved. Treatment would include oral Lactated Ringers Solution and some probiotics (i.e. Probiacin). A fecal examination may also be performed.

Resistance or reluctance to feed

This may be due to one or more of the following conditions:

- The animal is too weak or sick thereby having no interest in eating.

- The animal does not understand that you are offering food. Be sure to get a tiny taste in its mouth. This can sometimes require patience.

- The animal is too hot or cold.

- Your hands may be cold. Keep a warm cloth between you and the animal.

- You may be holding the animal too tightly or in an uncomfortable position.

- It may be too soon after the animal's last meal. If the stomach is still nicely full when you begin to feed, and the animal is not hungry enough to nurse well, lengthen the amount of time between feedings slightly.

SPECIES INFORMATION

MAMMAL

White-Tailed Deer

The white-tailed deer is named for its most distinctive feature, the large white tail or "flag" that is often all you see as the animal bounds away through tall grass. The color of the deer changes with the season, from a generally reddish-brown in the summer to a buff in winter. Its belly and the underside of its tail are completely white, and it has a white patch on the throat. A fawn's coat is similar to the adult's but has several hundred white spots which gradually disappear when the deer is three to four months old.

Fawns are born in late spring and summer and by early November a male fawn weighs about 85 pounds and a female about 80 pounds. Yearling bucks average 150 pounds, while does of the same age average about 20% less, or about 120 pounds. Some older bucks weigh 200 pounds or more.

Large "typical" bucks can have seven or more points on a side. Yearling bucks may have one to six points on each antler. Contrary to some opinions, numbers of points are no indication of age, but are some value in judging the animal's condition. Whitetails have developed keen senses to help them avoid predation. They depend on scent, particularly in thick cover, but also have excellent hearing and sight.

Weight	Males 150-200 pounds, Females are smaller
Antler growth	April to early May
Antler velvet shed	Early September
Antler shedding	January and February
Breeding season	Mid October-November
Gestation	7 months
Litter size	1-2 young
Birthing season	May-September
Fawn Birth Weight	Female 5.5 pounds, Males 7.5 pounds
	2-3 weeks old fawn will begin eating vegetation
Weaning	4 months
Maturity	2 years

Weight Calculation Chart

Girth	Weight
30	97
32	111
34	127
36	145
38	166
40	191
42	218
44	250
46	286

Opossum

Opossums are North America's only marsupial mammal (female has a pouch). They are solitary and nocturnal, usually slow moving and when frightened are unable to flee and fall into an involuntary shock-like state, "playing dead". They are very adaptable and are able to live wherever water, food, and shelter exists. When frightened they display their 50 sharp teeth and hiss; but in reality, they are gentle and placid, they prefer to avoid all confrontations.

Young are born after a brief gestation period of 12 days. Remarkably, the young climb into a pouch located on the female's abdomen. In the pouch, female opossums suckle and shelter their newborn young for almost 70 days. The young are completely weaned at about 100 days after entering their mothers pouch.

Opossums are omnivores and help to maintain a clean and healthy environment. They eat all types of insects, small rodents, plant matter, and over-ripe fruit. They even consume all types of carrion. They have an acute sense of hearing and smell but unfortunately have one of the smallest brain to body ratios among mammals.

Length	24-33 inches
Weight	6-12 pounds
Breeding season	February-April
Litter size	5-8; will have two litters a year
Gestation	12-13 days
Birthing season	Late February to late July
Nursing	The female nurses her young in her pouch until they are 2 months old, then they are carried on her back another month whenever they are away from the den.
Weaning	3-4 months old, around 7-9 inches long
Life expectancy	Up to 10 years

Raccoon

Raccoons are easily recognizable by their black mask and ringed tail. They vary in color from shades of brown, red or gray. Raccoons are primarily nocturnal but occasionally venture out in the daytime. In late fall and winter, raccoons may "den up" during the coldest periods; however, this is not true hibernation, and they will wander out during warm spells. The den is most often in a hollow tree, but raccoons will also use hollow logs, rock crevices, brush piles, buildings and abandoned woodchuck burrows, beaver lodges or fox dens. Adult males are territorial and may occupy an area of three to twenty square miles; females have a territory of one to six square miles. A raccoon's diet includes small mammals, small birds, crayfish, and plant matter.

Females produce one litter per year, with an average of four cubs per litter. The cubs are born blind, helpless and are covered with yellowish-gray fur. After five to seven weeks, the cubs leave the den and will travel with the female for short distances to search for food. At three to four months, the cubs begin to forage on their own. The cubs may stay with their mother until the following spring.

Length	20-40 inches long
Weight	12-35 pounds
Breeding season	February-May
Gestation	63 days
Litter size	3-5 young
Birthing season	April-June
Adult	10 months
Life expectancy	Up to 14 years

Eastern Cottontail Rabbit

Cottontail rabbits have large hind feet, long ears, and a short fluffy tail that resembles a cottonball. Their long coarse coat varies in color from reddish-brown to a black or grayish-brown. The underparts are white. Cottontails have excellent sight and hearing. They are active all year long, foraging mainly at night. Their habitat range varies, but generally the average is about three acres for females and eight acres for males. When frightened they can achieve speeds up to 18 mph over a short distance, often zigzagging to confuse a pursuing predator. One female cottontail rabbit and its offspring can reproduce 420 bunnies a year. Unfortunately they serve as a major food source for other animals and most cottontail rabbits do not live past three months of age.

Length	14-18 inches
Weight	2-3 pounds
Breeding season	March-September
Gestation	28-30 days
Litter size	3-8 young; will have 2-4 litters per year
Birthing season	Spring-Fall
Weaning	4 weeks
Life expectancy	Up to 4 years

Gray Squirrel

Squirrels are classified as members of the rodent order. The characteristics of rodents include a pair of long teeth at the front of both the upper and lower jaws. These teeth grow continuously throughout the squirrel's lifetime, constant gnawing on hard objects is a necessity in order to keep their teeth from growing too long. They have a well developed sense of smell which is important in locating their buried food; even in deep snow they are able to locate their stashes. Their great sense of smell also detects which nuts to harvest and which nuts are infested with insects that have bored into the nutritious center.

Gray squirrels build a type of nest, known as a drey, in the forms of trees. These consist mainly of dry leaves and twigs. They may use tree cavities during cold weather. Sometimes they will also attempt to build a nest in the attic or exterior walls of houses. Gray squirrels are known for invading bird feeders for millet and sunflower seeds, but safflower is often used instead, as they seem to have no taste for it. They have also been known to dig up bulbs from gardens.

Length	15 inches
Weight	1 pound
Breeding season	Late winter to early spring
Gestation	44-46 days
Litter size	4-6 young
Birthing season	Spring to mid-summer
Weaning	8-9 weeks
Maturity	10 months
Life expectancy	Up to 8 years

Woodchuck

How much wood could a woodchuck chuck if a woodchuck would chuck wood? The answer is 700 pounds. Woodchucks are excellent diggers, most burrows are 25-30 feet long and from two to five feet deep, with at least two entrances. The main entrance has a large mound of freshly dug dirt nearby, the other; less visible entrances are used for escape purposes. A nesting chamber for sleeping and raising the young is found at the end of the main tunnel. A separate toilet chamber helps keep the burrow clean. As cooler weather begins, woodchucks increase their feeding activity in order to produce a good layer of fat that is essential for a long hibernation. By the end of October, most woodchucks have begun their winter sleep. The woodchuck hibernates for four to five months. Respiration and overall metabolism rates while hibernating are greatly reduced and the animals are nourished from their fat reserves. Woodchucks come out from hibernation in February and March.

Length	16-20 inches
Weight	5-10 pounds
Breeding season	March-April
Gestation	28-32 days
Litter size	2-6 young
Birthing season	April-May
Weaning	5-6 weeks
Maturity	2 years
Life expectancy	Up to 7 years

Red Fox

The red fox looks much like a small dog with a pointed muzzle, long legs, large pointed ears and a bushy tail. A fox's dense fur allows it to curl up on the open ground and stay warm in even the coldest weather. Its tail is used to cover its nose and feet. They are most active at night, if seen during the daytime it will usually be late in the morning or early in the evening. About 60% of a red fox's diet is made up of rabbits and mice. They can run at speeds of more than 30 mph and are good swimmers. Red foxes rarely use dens except while raising their young. Young males travel an average of 25 miles from where they were born and can have a litter of their own at one year of age.

Length	36-46 inches
Weight	8-15 pounds
Breeding season	Late December to March
Gestation	49-56 days
Litter size	1-6 pups
Birthing season	Late March or early April
Reach adult size	7 months of age
Life expectancy	Up to 10 years

Coyote

The coyote is found throughout North America and are one of the most adaptable animals in the world. They can change their breeding habits, diet and social dynamics to survive in a wide variety of habitats. Coyotes can be recognized by their thick bushy tail, long pointy nose, and pointy ears. They can be told apart from their larger cousin the wolf and domestic dogs because coyotes carry their tail low when running whereas wolves and dogs carry their tail high.

Another way to distinguish between coyotes and dogs is the pattern of their tracks left in snow or soft mud. A coyote needs to conserve energy as it never knows where its next meal is coming from and so when it runs, it will place the back foot in the print made by the front foot, creating a single line of prints which tend to be straight and usually cross in open areas. Dogs tend to run with feet side by side, making two parallel sets of tracks which tend to meander in any direction. The tracks themselves are different too. The tracks of the front and back foot of a domestic dog are almost identical. In contrast, the front foot of a coyote is slightly larger than that of the back and the shape of the pad is different. The front pad is shaped like a frown and the back pad is shaped like lips.

Coyotes form loose family groups, not tight family packs like wolves. These groups may form for short periods, then break apart as food supply allows. When in large groups, they may occasionally work together in an attempt to catch a deer. Their main diet consists of small mammals, small birds, and carrion. Coyotes can run at a speed of 25-30 mph and can leap as far as 14 feet. They use at least ten different sounds to communicate, not counting their familiar yapping howl. Usually they call at night from an open area where the sound can travel up to three miles or more.

Length	40-60 inches
Weight	15-45 pounds
Breeding season	February-March
Gestation	63-65 days
Litter size	3-9 pups
Birthing season	April-May
Weaning	5-7 weeks
Reach adult size	1 year of age
Life expectancy	Up to 8 years

Brown Bat

The brown bat's fur color can range from pale tan to reddish or dark brown, and its ears and wings are dark brown to black. Bats are the only flying mammal; their wings contain bones similar to those in human arms and hands. They have a unique skill called "echolocation" which makes them able to detect something as fine as a human hair in total darkness. As a bat flies about searching for food it is usually making 10 to 50 calls a second. Brown bats are insectivorous; they feed on insects such as moths, beetles, mosquitoes, and flies. A single bat can consume 600 mosquitoes or more in just one hour. Bats hunt for about two hours after sunset and two more hours just before sunrise. Between hunts, the bats rest in roosts or crevices and form tight clusters.

During the summer months, the bats consume about half their weight in insects each night. This enables them to put on the body fat needed to survive months of hibernation. Bats will crawl into small crevices or hook their claws into ceilings. Then hang upside down and go into a state of deep hibernation. While in this deep sleep, all body functions are affected; the heart rate slows to twenty beats per minute, respiration decreases, and the body temperature drops to within one degree of the surrounding air temperature. These bats can now survive six to eight months on very little energy. The bats will wake up occasionally to urinate, drink, and mate. Uninterrupted sleep for brown bats averages between twelve and nineteen days but may last as long as 93 days. Moisture from cave walls and condensation droplets on their fur are the usual source of water during hibernation.

Length	3-3.5 inches
Weight	0.3-0.5 ounces
Wing span	6-8 inches
Gestation	50-60 days
Litter size	1 pup per year, may have twins
Birthing season	May to July
Weaning	30 days
Maturity	Females 6-9 months; Males 12-16 months
Life Expectancy	Up to 30 years

Striped Skunk

The striped skunk is a member of the Mustelid family, which includes weasel, mink and otter. They are about the size of a small house cat and its fur is mostly black with white on top of the head and neck. In most animals the white extends down the back, usually separating into two white stripes. Skunks are nocturnal, hunting at night for insects, grub, small rodents, snakes, frogs, fruit, pet food, bird food, and garbage. Skunks are slow moving and docile, their senses of sight, hearing, and smell are poor compared to many predators.

When they feel threatened they arch their back and raise their tail while stamping their front feet on the ground. If this warning is ignored by the intruder then the skunk will turn around and with its tail raised, discharge an obnoxious musk. This musk is secreted by two internal glands located at the base of the tail. The glands open to the outside through small nipples which are hidden when the tail is down and exposed when it's raised. A skunk has voluntary control over the glands and can control the direction in which the musk is discharged. They can accurately spray their target up to ten feet or more. The glands contain about one tablespoon of thick, volatile, yellowish, oily liquid. This musk has been detected at distances up to twenty miles away from where it was discharged.

Length	20-30 inches
Weight	3-11.7 pounds
Breeding season	February-March
Gestation	62-72 days
Litter size	4-10 young, with an average of 6
Birthing season	May-June
Reach adult size	10 months of age
Life expectancy	Up to 6 years

Thirteen-Lined Ground Squirrel

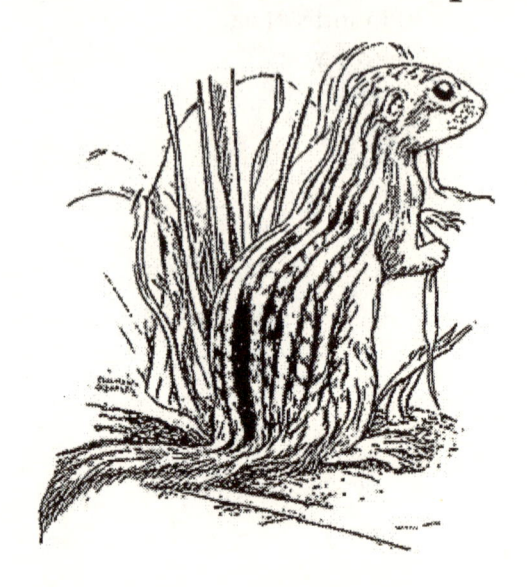

This squirrel has thirteen light stripes with rows of light spots that run the length of its back. The background color is tan or brown and the belly is white. Its color pattern blends into its surroundings, protecting it from predators. They dig burrows that are 15 to 20 feet long and often have more than one entrance. Their home range is two to three acres. Grass, weed seeds, caterpillars, and grasshoppers are its dietary staples but it sometimes will eat bird flesh and even mice and shrews. The thirteen-lined ground squirrel sometimes damages gardens by digging burrows and eating vegetables, but also devours weed seeds and harmful insects. It often stands upright to survey its domain, diving down into its burrow when it senses danger. It has a maximum running speed of 8 mph.

In late summer, they will put on a heavy layer of fat and store some food in their burrows. They will enter their nest in October, roll into a stiff ball, and decrease their respiration as they go into hibernation. Hibernation will last approximately 240 days, and then they emerge from their burrows in March or early April. Males arise from hibernation before the females and soon begin their search for available females to breed.

Length	body 225 mm; tail length 75-109 mm
Weight	4-5 ounces
Breeding season	Females mate within 5 days of spring emergence from hibernation
Gestation	28 days
Litter size	7-10 young
Weaning	6 weeks
Reach adult size	9 months
Life expectancy	Up to 2 years

SPECIES INFORMATION

AVIAN

Great Egret

The great egret is a member of the heron family, with long legs, white plumage, and a slender body. Adults have black legs and feet. During the breeding season the normally yellow bill may appear orange and long feather plumes extend from the back to beyond the tail. Immature egrets and non-breeding adults have no plumes and the color of their bills and legs are duller. Nests are built 20 to 40 feet above ground in trees and constructed of sticks and twigs and lined with plant material. Their diet consists of fish, crayfish, amphibians, aquatic insects, crickets, grasshoppers, and mice.

Length	38 inches
Weight	32-40 ounces
Wingspan	55 inches
Breeding season	Mid April
Clutch	4-5 oval, smooth, greenish-blue eggs
Incubation	23-24 days
Fledge	3-4 weeks
Life expectancy	Up to 22 years

Great Blue Heron

The Great Blue Heron is the largest heron in North American and is also the most well-known and most widespread heron in the continent. This heron has a blue-gray back, black sides and a gray and white striped belly. They are easily recognized in flight by their six foot wingspan and their long neck which is folded and held in the shape of an "S" while in flight. Their diet consists mainly of fish, amphibians, snakes, crayfish, small rodents, and large insects. They forage for their food by using their long legs to wade in the shallow waters, where they walk slowly or stand still and then strike quickly with their "spear like" bill to catch their food.

Length	3 feet
Height	4 feet
Wingspan	6 feet
Breeding season	March-May
	Southern range November-April
Clutch size	3-5 greenish-blue eggs
Incubation	27 days by both parents
Fledge	53 days
Life expectancy	Up to 17 years

Snowy Egret

The snowy egret is also known as the lesser egret, little egret, and little white heron. The snowy egret is a medium-sized heron with a slender body, black bill, black legs, and yellow feet. The area of the upper bill, in front of the eyes, is yellow but turns red during the breeding season. While feeding in shallow areas of ponds and marshes, snowy egrets use one foot to stir up the bottom, flushing their prey into view. Some snowy egrets will hover and then drop to the water to catch their prey with their bills.

Length	20-27 inches
Weight	13 ounces
Wingspan	41 inches
Breeding season	Mid April
Clutch	3-4 oval, greenish-blue eggs
Incubation	23-24 days
Fledge	3-4 weeks
Life expectancy	Up to 16 years

Herring Gull

The herring gull is considered your basic "seagull"; it has no distinctive characters that set it apart from other gull species. Its plumage is gray and the head is white with a yellow beak. The coloring of the legs may vary from reddish to yellowish. Immature individuals have dark brown coloring, darker beak, and brown legs.

The herring gull regularly drinks fresh water when it is available. If there is none, the gull will drink seawater. Special glands located over its eyes allow it to excrete the salt. The salty excretion can be seen dripping out of the gull's nostrils and off the end of its bill. The herring gull's diet consists of fish, invertebrates, mollusks, refuse, small mammals, birds, and vegetable matter.

Length	22-26 inches
Wingspan	54-57 inches
Weight	28-44 ounces
Clutch	2-3 eggs
Incubation	25-33 days
Fledge	6 weeks
Maturity	3-4 years
Life expectancy	Up to 30 years

Mallard Duck

The mallard is probably one of the most easily recognized ducks. Mallards are dabbling ducks and feed by tipping forward to submerge their heads and necks. The male or "drake" is recognized by its glossy, green head and white neck-ring. It has a yellow bill, rusty breast, and white tail. The female is brown with an orange-yellow bill and whitish tail. Both have orange feet and blue speculum (patch on their wing) framed with a white bar on each side. It nests mainly near water, in vegetation. The eggs are incubated by the female and once hatched; the young are looked after by her as well. When the young reach seven to eight weeks of age they will be able to fly.

Length	20-26 inches
Weight	3-3.5 pounds
Wing span	30-40 inches
Breeding season	Late winter-spring
Clutch size	8-12 greenish-buff colored eggs
Incubation	26 days
Fledge	8 weeks
Maturity	1 year
Life expectancy	Up to 4 years

Canada Goose

Although they are named for Canada, Canada geese are found all over North America. There are as many as 11 different races of Canada geese. They travel in long strings in V formation, announcing their presence by honking. Their nests are made in a hollow in the ground and lined with plant matter and down feathers. Canada geese generally mate for life, and both parents take part in aggressively protecting goslings. The goslings will usually stay with their parents for one year. Should one mate die, the other mate may not pair-bond again for years, and some mates may remain single for the rest of their life.

Length	22-45 inches
Wing span	50-68 inches
Weight	13-15 pounds
Breeding season	Late winter-spring
Clutch size	4-8 white eggs
Incubation	28 days
Maturity	2-3 years
Life expectancy	Up to 8 years

Barn Owl

Barn owls have a white, heart-shaped facial disk, no ear tufts and long legs. They appear white from below and golden-brown from above with black specks all over. Barn owls are monogamous (one mate). They do not construct a nest; the eggs are laid in a dark space surrounded by pellets. These brownish-black pellets, which are the regurgitated fur and bone fragments of each meal, average about two inches in size and are produced twice daily. Owls are primarily nocturnal birds belonging to the order of Strigiformes.

Length	Males 13-15 inches; Females 14-20 inches
Wing span	Males 41-45 inches; Females 43-47 inches
Weight	Males 14-19 ounces; Females 17-25 ounces
Breeding season	April
Clutch	5-11 eggs, average being 4-6
Incubation	30-34 days
Maturity	1 year
Life expectancy	Up to 12 years

Short-Eared Owl

Short-eared owls have small ear tufts that appear as two ridges along the top of their head. They have a round, beige facial disk similar to that of a barn owl. The underparts are a buffy-white in males or a tawny-rust in females, with bold streaks of brown. These birds primarily eat small rodents. It often comes to rest on the ground and usually flies low. They are diurnal; often observed in the late afternoon and at dawn or dusk. Its voice can be compared to the nasal bark of a dog, sounds like kee-aw or boo-boo-boo. An interesting fact about owls is that they can turn their head 270 degrees and quickly swivel it back in the opposite direction making it appear that it is turning its head in a circle.

Length	13-17 inches
Wing span	38-44 inches
Weight	Males 11 ounces; Females 13 ounces
Breeding season	Late April
Clutch	4-8 eggs are short, oval, smooth, and non-glossy
Incubation	24-28 days
Maturity	1 year
Life expectancy	Up to 12 years

Long-Eared Owl

Adult long-eared owls have a slender, gray-brown body and a bold breast with vertical streaks. The ear tufts, located near the center of the head, are long and blackish. This owl also has a rusty facial disk edged with black and gray, a gray-black bill and yellow eyes. Owls have no crop and since they lack this, food is passed directly into their digestive system. Several hours after eating, the indigestible parts (fur, bones, teeth and feathers that are still in the gizzard) are compressed into a pellet the same shape as the gizzard. This pellet travels up from the gizzard back to the proventriculus. It will remain there for up to 10 hours before being regurgitated. Because the stored pellet blocks the owl's digestive system, new prey cannot be swallowed until the pellet is ejected.

Length	13-16 inches
Wing span	36-42 inches
Weight	Males 8.6 ounces; Females 10 ounces
Breeding season	4-5 glossy, white eggs
Incubation	25-30 days
Maturity	1 year
Life expectancy	Up to 30 years

Red-Tailed Hawk

Red-tailed hawks are stocky birds that are brown with a white breast and a rust-colored tail. Immature red-tailed hawks are dull in color, have more streaks, and are missing the rust color in their tail. When the young are approaching two years of age their tails will begin to change color and have their traditional red color. Red-tailed hawks are seen the most because of their habit of circling high up in the air or found perching along the road on telephone poles. They have excellent eyesight; eight times more powerful than ours. They can spot a mouse from a height of 100 feet. Red-tailed hawks are very territorial; a pair will aggressively protect their territory which ranges from one-half to two square miles.

Length	17-22 inches
Wing span	43-56 inches
Weight	2-4 pounds
Breeding season	Spring
Clutch	3-5 eggs
Incubation	30-34 days
Maturity	3 years
Life expectancy	Up to 20 years

American Kestrel

The American kestrel is the most common of the small falcons in North America. It is often called the Sparrow Hawk, a misnomer as it is neither a sparrow nor a hawk. Males have slate blue wings and broad black bands on a gray tail. Females are rust colored on both their backs and wings and have a banded tail. American kestrels build their nests in a hollow in a tree or on ledges of a building. The female mainly incubates the eggs. The nestlings are able to fly at about thirty days after hatching. Their diet consists of insects, mice, and small birds.

Length	8.5 inches
Weight	3.5-4.5 ounces
Breeding season	March
Clutch	3-5 eggs
Incubation	27-33 days
Fledge	27-34 days
Life expectancy	Up to 13 years

Peregrine Falcon

The Peregrine falcon has dark gray-blue or dark brown upper parts and reddish-white lower parts, with close black bars. The female is larger and darker with more barred areas in the lower parts. These birds nests in rocks, rarely in trees. The eggs are incubated by both sexes. The young are able to fly 35-42 days after hatching and stay with their parents for another two months. Their diet consists of birds and small mammals. The peregrine falcon is best known for its spectacular method of capturing prey in mid-air. When hunting it increases its speed in the air by making aerial dives with its wings partially or fully pulled in. The peregrine plunges at speeds up to 175 mph to attack its prey, which is killed instantly. Normal flight speed can range between 28-60 mph.

Length	15-20 inches
Wing span	43-46 inches
Weight	1.5-2.5 pounds
Breeding season	Spring
Clutch	3-4 buff-colored eggs covered with red-brown markings laid in April-May
Incubation	28-29 days
Maturity	3 years
Life expectancy	Up to 20 years

Mourning Dove

Doves are members of the columbidae family and are found all over the world. Male and female mourning doves look very similar with grayish-brown backs, buff-colored undersides, black spots on the wings and behind the eye, and white feathers in the tail, which show during flight. Juveniles can be distinguished from adults by light buffing on the tips of the primary feathers which persist until the first molt.

Doves are monogamous, they pair for life. The male leads the female to potential nest sites. The female will build the nest while the male will gather material and bring it to her. The nests are made of twigs and grass usually placed in trees or shrubs ten to thirty feet above ground. Both sexes will incubate the eggs; the nest is very rarely left unattended by the pair. Like members of the parrot family, doves and pigeons have something called a "true crop". This means that they have the ability to produce a thick substance known as "crop milk", which they regurgitate for their young. Most of an adult dove's diet consist of weed seeds and grains. Insects make up a very small portion of their diet.

Length	10.5-12 inches
Clutch size	2 white eggs
Incubation	14 days
Fledge	14 days
Maturity	1½ years
Life expectancy	Up to 31 years

Pigeon

Pigeons may have been the first bird species to be domesticated. There are as many as 28 pigeon color types. Pigeons have colorful, iridescent neck feathers which are called a hackle. Adult males and females look alike, but a male's hackle is more iridescent than a female's. Pigeons have many types of feathers, some of which are accompanied by one or two filoplume feathers that look like hairs. These filoplumes may have sensory functions, such as detecting touch and pressure changes. Adults have orange or reddish orange eyes. Juveniles that are less than six to eight months old have medium brown or grayish brown eyes. A pigeon's eyesight is excellent and can see color, even ultraviolet light, part of the light spectrum that human's can't see. Pigeons can hear sounds at much lower frequencies than humans can, such as wind blowing across buildings and mountains, distant thunderstorms and even far-away volcanoes. Sensitive hearing may explain why pigeons sometimes fly away for no apparent reason.

Their drinking behavior is unique, while most birds take a sip of water and throw back their heads to let the water trickle down their throats, pigeons suck up water using their beaks like straws. Pigeons form small flocks of around twenty to thirty birds. There is usually an even number of males and females. Seeds, fruits, and grains make up the bulk of their diet.

A pigeon nest is usually constructed with small twigs and located on covered building ledges that resemble cliffs. The male brings the nesting material to his mate, one piece at a time and she builds the nest, usually well-hidden and hard to find. Pigeons reproduce throughout the year, even during winter, and can raise four to five broods annually. Both parents take turns keeping the eggs warm. Males usually stay on the nest during the day; females at night. The young are fed crop milk for about the first two weeks. Crop milk is a specially produced secretion that both parents produce from the lining of the crop, a sac-like food storage chamber that projects outward from the bottom of the esophagus.

Pigeons can reach a flight speed of 15 to 60 miles per hour and may fly as far as 600 miles a day.

Length	11-13 inches
Weight	8-13 ounces
Breeding season	Spring and fall but may reproduce year round
Clutch size	1-2 eggs
Incubation	16-19 days
Independent	6-8 weeks
Life expectancy	Up to 26 years

Robin

Robins have brown on their backs, orange on their breast, and white on their lower belly and under their tail feathers. Their throats are white with streaks of black and have white rings around their eyes. Females are slightly paler in color than males. Young robins have dark spots on their breasts and are also paler in color than adult males.

Robins are most active during the day. They are social birds, especially during the winter when they are gathered in large numbers on their winter grounds. They assemble in large flocks at night where they roost in the trees. Robins defend breeding territories during the summer and are less social during that time. Young robins remain in the area of their nest for their first four months of life. They gather in mixed-age flocks when it becomes time to depart for their winter grounds. Almost all populations of robins are migratory.

Robins are monogamous; males and females form a pair bond and stay together during breeding season and while raising their young. Robins breed in the spring shortly after returning from their winter migration. They are one of the first birds to begin laying eggs and have two to three clutch's each season. Female robins build a cup-shaped nest made of long coarse grass, twigs, feathers and paper. The inside is lined with mud that she smears with her breast and later fills with finer pieces of grass to cushion the eggs. Robins mostly build their nest five to fifteen feet above ground in dense bushes, trees, on window ledges, or above doorways. A new nest is made for each clutch. After the eggs have hatched the female continues to feed the chicks. The young robins leave the nest in two weeks after they have hatched. Even after leaving the nest the young robins are followed by their parents who feed them and distract predators until they are able to fly which will take another two weeks.

Length	10 inches
Weight	63-103 grams
Wing span	4.7-5.4 inches
Breeding season	April-July
Clutch	3-6 blue eggs; will have 2 clutches a year
Incubation	12-14 days
Fledge	14-16 days
Sexually mature	1 year
Life expectancy	Up to 14 years

American Crow

Adult American crows are completely black in color; in the sunlight the feathers have a glossy purplish iridescent look. The bill is black with a slight hook on the end of it and stiff bristles cover their nostrils. Juvenile crows are about the same size as adults; they have blue eyes and the inside of their mouths are pink.

Most crows defend a large all-purpose territory. Members of the family assist in chasing predators away from their territories. In addition to family groups, crows may join a third kind of social group called a floater flock. During the breeding season, floater flocks of up to 50 birds have been observed. Flock participants probably lack mates; some of these individuals may spend time in their natal territories as helpers, staying close to the place where they were born helps them raise the young and defend their territory against predators. Non-breeders or helpers from a territory may leave for a while in the winter and return in the spring. It is not understood why these offspring do not obtain mates and raise their own families, but pairs with helpers do not appear to be more successful at raising offspring than those without helpers.

If a floater flock were to become a breeder it can either leave the territory to establish it's own, wait for another crow in the neighborhood to die and then take its territory, or it can take over a portion of their parents' territory or inherit it when the parent birds die.

During breeding season when the female is incubating her eggs, after they have hatched, the female will beg for food like a baby bird and her mate will bring it to her. Each breeding pair has an established home territory averaging about ten acres. Crows will group together and vocally harass and chase predators away, this behavior is called mobbing. Crows rebuild their nests every year in a different location but will stay in the family territory.

Crows are highly vocal birds; they have a complex system of loud, harsh caws that are often uttered in repetitive rhythmic series. Shorter and sharper caws are probably alarm or alert calls. Slightly longer caws are probably used in territorial defense. Double short caws repeated in stereotype, may serve as a call-to-arms vocalization, alerting family members to territorial intruders. Harsher cawing is used while mobbing potential predators. Softer coos that crows can make accompanied by bowing postures are used among family members possibly as a greeting.

Length	16-18 inches
Weight	1 pound
Wing span	39 inches
Breeding season	February-June; one brood per year
Clutch	4-5 light green colored eggs with brown markings
Incubation	18 days
Fledge	35 days
Sexually mature	2 years of age
Life expectancy	Up to 14 years

House Sparrow

Although House Sparrows belong to a different family of birds, they closely resemble North American sparrows. They are short and stocky with shorter legs and thicker bills than native sparrows. The back is brown with black streaking. The breast and belly are unstreaked dull gray. Males in breeding plumage have a gray crown, with chestnut bordering the crown and extending down the back of the neck. The cheek and side of the neck is white. A black bib extends to the throat and meets the black stripe in front of the eye. The bill is dark gray black, and the legs are pale brown. The rump is gray, the shoulders are chestnut, and the wings are brownish with a white wing bar. The tail is dusky gray brown. Fall and winter males may lack the bright colors and black bib.

Females have a grayish brown crown and have a grayish buff eye stripe. They lack the chestnut and black colors of the male, and their upperparts and wings are much grayer than the male. The back is light brown with black streaks; the rest of the head, breast, and sides are grayish brown. The belly is dull white. The bill and legs are pale brown. Immature males resemble females, except for the darker crown and a faint grayish bib.

The breeding season for House Sparrows begins early in the spring or even in midwinter, and each pair may produce up to four broods a season. Although they usually prefer to nest in a cavity, House Sparrows will settle for any nook or cranny they can find. The nest is a large, untidy ball of grass, wool and feathers, lined with feathers and finer plant material.

They are not migratory birds, but flocks of birds may move about within a two mile radius. House Sparrows are primarily seed-eaters, although they eat some insects during the summer. Farmsteads are particularly attractive to sparrows as they provide an abundant source of food, as well as shelter and plenty of nesting sites.

Length	4.3-5.7 inches
Weight	26-32 grams
Wing span	7-10 inches
Breeding season	Early spring or even mid-winter
Clutch	3-5 white/brown speckled eggs
Incubation	11-14 days
Fledge	14-16 days
Life expectancy	Up to 13 years

Starling

European Starlings are stocky birds with short, square-tipped tails and pointed wings. Both sexes are iridescent black. The sheen is mostly green-tinted on the back, breast, and belly; mixed green and purple on the crown; and purple on the nape and throat. Body feathers have creamy or white triangular terminal markings that are lost through wear so that by breeding season, adults are entirely glossy black, without white spots. First-year birds are more heavily spotted than adults. Following the breeding season, in late summer and fall, the yellow bill darkens to brownish gray or black in almost all birds.

The sexes are very similar with only a few differences in detail. The male's eyes are uniformly brown, whereas the female's eyes have is a lighter ring around the outer edge. A female's bill is pinkish at the base of the lower mandible whereas a male's bill is bluish or blue gray. The underwing coverts are black in males and brown or gray in females. In the spring, the bill of the starling is yellow, but it becomes dark in the winter.

Starlings are highly social birds. At any time of the year, they can be found feeding, migrating or roosting in flocks. The winter flock shown here, consisting of at least 3,000 birds, was located in downtown Indianapolis. Starlings have a well developed sense of taste, and are repelled by grape flavoring. Fogging with grape flavoring is an effective an environmentally safe method to discourage these birds from roosting.

Starlings are cavity nesters, and will use a natural cavity in a tree, a woodpecker hole, an opening in a building, a ventilation pipe or a nest box. The nest, started by the male before pairing, is made of leaves, stems, and other plant material. The nest is kept fastidiously clean at first, but is allowed to get dirty and riddled with nest parasites before the young birds fledge.

Length	7.5-9 inches
Weight	2.5-3 ounces
Wing span	13-16 inches
Breeding season	January-August
Clutch	5-7 pale blue-green eggs
Incubation	12-15 days
Fledge	20-22 days
Sexually mature	2 years
Life expectancy	Up to 20 years

BASIC HOUSING REQUIREMENTS FOR ANIMALS/AVIANS

(W x L x H)

Animal	Infant	Nursing	Juvenile	Injured Adult
Deer	4x4x4	10x10x6	30x60x6	8x8x8
Opossum	10 Gal.	2x3x2	4x4x8	2x2x2
Raccoon	20 Gal.	2x3x4	6x6x6	2x3x3
Cottontail Rabbit	10 Gal.	20 Gal.	4x6x4	2x2x2
Squirrel	10 Gal.	20 Gal.	4x4x6	4x4x4
Woodchuck	20 Gal.	2x4x3	6x8x6	4x4x4
Fox	2x2x2	3x3x3	4x4x8	4x4x4
Coyote	2x2x2	3x3x3	8x8x6	4x4x4
Skunk	20 Gal.	2x4x3	6x6x6	3x3x3
Ground Squirrel	10 Gal.	2x3x2	4x4x6	2x2x2

		Restricted Activity	Limited Activity	Unlimited Activity
Doves, Pigeons		12"x18"x12"	12"x20"x16"	12'x8'x8'
Songbirds	<5"	8"x12"x8"	12"x18"x8"	2'x4'x4'
	>5"	12"x12"x12"	18"x18"x18"	4'x8'x8'
Crows	<17"	14"x18"x18"	24"x18"x24"	8'x16'x8
	>17"	16"x22"x22"	2'x2'x2'	10'x30'x15'
Egrets/Herons	<20"	18"x18"x18"	3'x3'x3'	4'x12'x8'
	>20"	3'x3'x4'	4'x8'x4'	10'x26'x10'
Gulls	<14"	12"x16"x18"	20"x24"x18"	6'x12'x8'
	>14"	18"x20"x18"	2'x2'x2'	8'x15'x8'
Ducks		18"x20"x18"	2'x2'x2'	8'x10'x8'
Geese		4'x3'x3'	4'x6'x4'	10'x16'x8'
Barn Owl		16"x28"x24"	6'x8'x8'	10'x30'x12'
Short-Eared Owl		16"x28"x24"	6'x8'x8'	10'x30'x12'
Long-Eared Owl		16"x28"x24"	6'x8'x8'	10'x30'x12'
Red-Tailed Hawk		16"x28"x24"	6'x8'x8'	10'x50'x10'
American Kestrel		16"x24"x22"	6'x8'x8'	8'x16'x10'
Peregrine Falcon		3'x3'x4'	8'x8'x8'	20'x99'x15'

HOUSING FOR BIRDS

Housing an orphan or injured bird varies due to the age of the bird. Minimal handling and a warm quiet environment away from other animals is best in order to keep the amount of stress down. Here are several examples of enclosures you can use.

Nestling

You can use a cardboard box; place a round bowl with tissues torn up in it as a temporary nest and housing unit. Place a heating pad underneath the box set on low. Cover the top with a towel to keep the light out, the heat in, and place in a quiet area as to reduce the amount of stress the little one may be going through. You can use small plastic carriers that are made for hamsters or guinea pigs and line the bottom with nesting material and be able to place a heating pad underneath the carrier set on low to keep the nestling warm. Keep a thermometer in the box or carrier in order to monitor the temperature inside the enclosure which should be around 85 to 90 degrees.

Fledgling

A bird cage with small bars, as used for parakeets, will work well temporarily. It is important that the fledgling can not manage to get through the bars. You can also use a small pet carrier if you're in a pinch. Line the carrier with paper towels or newspapers for easy cleaning. You can use towels but make sure there are no strings hanging off of them that may cause the bird to get tangled up. You can design a nest of tissues torn up in a small box or bowl until the fledgling is ready to move onto perching.

Make sure there's plenty of room to perch, explore, and flap wings. As the bird gets older it will need to practice grasping things and perching on branches. They also start stretching out their wings and may frequently lose their balance while perching, so make sure it's not a long drop to the floor. Once they learn how to use their wings, it is time to move them to a larger outdoor aviary. Here they will gain strength, learn to maneuver, and get used to their outdoor environment and the sounds around them.

Something to keep in mind when housing any bird that you are going to eventually release back into the environment, avoid imprinting upon them. Do not let the bird get used to human contact, sounds, television, telephone, controlled lighting, temperature, the family dog or cat, etc. It is crucial to their survival that minimal handling and contact occurs. The best place to house them is outdoors, as well as you can keep them safe from predators.

HOME-MADE INCUBATORS

Home-made incubator with heating pad

You will need a clear plastic storage container the size used for storing shoes or even one that is a little bigger; it all depends on the size and number of infants that will need to be placed in the incubator.

You will need to drill air holes in the lid.

Place a towel under the container and a heating pad set on low.

Place another towel inside the incubator, preferably one without strings or holes in it so the infant's nails do not get caught up in it. A wee-wee pad works good too.

A thermometer should be placed inside the incubator to keep track of the temperature. The temperature should be maintained at 90 degrees.

Place the air hole lid on top of container to prevent escape and keep heat in.

Home-made incubator with water heater

You will need two of the same sized clear plastic storage containers. The size used for storing shoes or even a little bigger is good; it all depends on the size and number of infants that will need to be placed in the incubator.

You will need to drill air holes in one of the lids, the other lid you will not use.

Fill one of the containers with water about 2" or more, it needs to be enough to cover the water heater that will then be placed on the bottom of the container.

Place a 100-watt submersible aquarium heater in the water, set to 100 degrees.

Place the second container into the first container that is filled with water. Get any air-bubbles out from under the container that is contacting the water with the heater in it by tilting to one side.

Place a towel inside the incubator, preferably one without strings or holes in it so the infant's nails do not get caught up in it. A wee-wee pad works good too.

A thermometer should be placed inside the incubator to keep track of the temperature. The temperature should be maintained at 90 degrees.

Place the air hole lid on top of container to prevent escape and keep heat in.

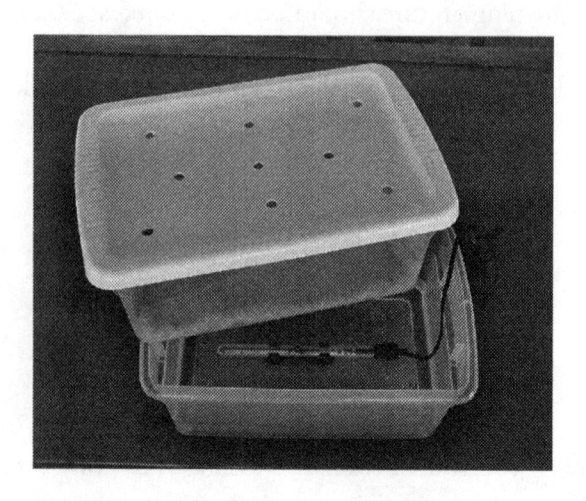

PERSONAL SAFETY

Your personal safety is the first thing you should consider when handling an injured wildlife situation. It's instinctual for animals to fear humans and when they are injured they will react to that fear. If you are injured by an animal's beak, teeth or claws you will be of little help.

For injured birds, gently wrap them in a cloth as you pick them up. This gives you a better grip and helps keep the wings and/or legs from further damage as it struggles. It's also a good idea to cover the bird's eyes. If it can't see you, it has less reason to be scared.

If you should have to handle a baby animal you should protect your hands by wearing thick gloves. Do not try handling adult raccoons, opossums, deer or any large bird. Contact someone who is a wildlife rehabilitator or animal care specialist familiar with that species so they can send a trained person with appropriate equipment.

If an injured animal is in the middle of the road and you need to assist it immediately, do so with extreme caution. Defensive reactions by such animals can cause great harm to you. A heron will go straight for the eyes and can blind or kill you with its sharp, powerful beak. A deer can break a rib or cause even more damage if it kicks you. A raccoon may grab and bite at you multiple times. It's not that these animals are naturally aggressive, these animals are scared and in pain. They cannot run away so they will defend themselves anyway they can. Don't assume that the animals understand that you are trying to help them.

Use proper equipment when handling animals. Welder's gloves work well when handling most wildlife. Have extra towels handy, cages open and ready, a fishing net (depends on species) available for quick capture should it get away from you. Also wear goggles to protect your eyes when handling certain species such as herons or other animals that may cause damage to your eyes. Have latex gloves available to wear for the exam, transferring or cleaning up after the animal. You want to avoid direct contact with any animals' feces, urine, saliva, vomit or other microscopic organism that may be a health risk to you.

When washing towels used for wildlife, use bleach in the wash. Use disinfectants in cages and areas where wildlife is kept that kills diseases that they may be transmitting. Read labels for any disinfectant or detergent for proper mixing, usage, and safety issues.

RESCUE AND HANDLING

If you spot an animal that you feel may need assistance, do not catch it right away. Take 20 minutes or so to observe its behavior. In the case of a young animal, it may simply be waiting for a parent to return. Adult animals will often leave their young to hunt for food and return within a short period of time to feed and care for the offspring.

If you believe the animal is orphaned or injured, call a rehabilitation center near you before you pick up the animal. An animal you think is orphaned may not really be abandoned and an injured wild animal can be dangerous and need special handling. Keep an eye on its whereabouts and describe its condition to the rehabilitator you reach on the phone. They will give you the proper course of action to take for that particular animal.

If, however, you are unable to reach a rehabilitation center for advice, a good rule of thumb is to wear appropriate clothing and safety equipment. Use common sense and wear gloves and eye protection when attempting to handle a wild animal.

The best thing to do if you find a baby bird is to leave it alone, the parent birds may be watching nearby. If the bird appears as though it has fallen from a nest, try to locate the nest and carefully return the baby bird.

If the bird has feathers, it may be a fledged bird and a parent bird is probably close by. As long as the bird is in no danger from cats or other predators, it is best to watch the bird from a distance to see if a parent returns. Watch the activity of the baby bird for an hour or so before determining that the bird needs human assistance.

If the bird is small or very young you can pick it up very gently with a washcloth. Do not constrict it's breathing by holding it too tight, carefully control any thrashing around or flapping of its wings to prevent any further injury.

For birds such as crows, throw a dishtowel over them and grasp them with two hands around the wings and hold the bird out in front of you. This tactic works the best with birds, throwing a towel over the bird will prevent it from flapping its wings which may cause injury to itself, plus the darkness will calm it down. Transfer the bird to a suitably sized box where it can be fed and cared for properly.

For birds such as ducks or geese, throw a blanket or sheet over the bird and grasp them over the wings to keep them from flapping, keep their head tucked under your arm to keep them from thrashing around. Do not apply to much pressure around the bird or hold the towel or sheet around them too tight as this may constrict their breathing.

If you are unable to catch the bird and you find yourself chasing it around then it probably does not need rescuing. Discontinue your rescue attempt as the stress of you chasing it may worsen its condition or even kill it.

PHYSICAL EXAM

First you should prepare for the examination. Get the supplies you will need set-up, including towels, antiseptic wash, saline solution, bandage material, and scissors. Have everything that you may need available, in your reach, should you need it.

Stress is high in animals being transported to your care and they should be kept in a quiet, warm, dark area so they may calm down. You should observe the animal while it is resting quietly. Observe for neurological signs, can the animal stand, is there any blood or discharge from anywhere, and does it appear weak and disoriented? Watch respirations and listen to sounds you may hear coming from the animal.

Keep noise, activities, and handling to a minimum to reduce stress and discontinue the exam should the animal become distressed.

Start your exam from the head and work your way down to the legs.

Eye Exam

- Any discharge, if so what color is it. (i.e. clear, green, brown)
- Are the pupils equal, dilated, constricted?
- How do they react to a light source?
- Is there any nystagmus (eyes move quickly from side to side, twitching)
- Any blood, abrasions, cuts in or around the eye?
- Do they appear sunken in?
- Is there any fowl odor?

Ear Exam

- Any discharge, redness or swelling?
- Any external parasites?
- Any foreign body lodged in the ear canal?

Mouth Exam

- Are the gums and tongue pink or what color is normal for that species?
- Are there any loose, broken or missing teeth?
- Are there any lesions in or around the mouth?
- Are the teeth overgrown, does the mouth close properly?
- Is there any fowl odor?

Nose Exam

- Any nasal discharge, if so what color? (i.e. clear, green, red)
- How does the animal sound while breathing?
- Any cuts, abrasions, or lesions?

In birds with crops note if the crop is empty, has partial substance in it or full.

Overall body condition of animal/avian

- Any cuts, abrasions, bald spots, punctures or missing feathers?
- Any hotspots, rashes or infection/puss anywhere on the skin?
- Any external parasites?
- Does it look or feel thin?
- Do the limbs appear swollen and are there any fractures?
- Do the extremities feel cold?
- Does the pulse seem weak?
- Does the abdomen feel or look distended?
- Is it breathing fast, slow, panting, or shallow?
- Does the animal have anal tone?
- Does the skin color appear normal or jaundice?

Hydration Exam

- Is the animal dehydrated?
- Check by pulling up the skin between the shoulder blade area or down the middle of the back and release. It should return to normal right away, should it go back very slowly or tent up then you can be sure the animal is dehydrated.
- In birds their eyes will appear sunken in and less bright if they are dehydrated.
- In larger birds, the skin over their toes can be gently pulled up and observed to return to a normal position.

Stethoscope Exam

- Listen to the heart and lungs. Remember to listen to the left and right side of the thorax. Do you hear any abnormalities?
- Count the number of heart beats in 15 seconds and multiply by 4 to get an average beat per minute. Rates increase with excitement or temperature.
- Count the number of respirations in 15 seconds and multiply by 4 to get an average respiratory rate per minute.

Other

- Any diarrhea or vomiting?
- Is it urinating normally, straining, or urinating more frequently?
- With birds, their stool and urates are mixed in the droppings. The stool portion is dark and more solid; the urates are runnier in texture and should be white in color.
- Is the animal/bird interested in eating or drinking?

WILDLIFE ADMISSION FORM

Date: _____ Species: _____ Case #: ___ - _____

Sex: _____ Age: _____ Weight: _____

↓TO BE FILLED OUT BY PERSON PRESENTING ANIMAL OR BIRD↓

Name: _____ Phone #: _____

Address: _____

City: _____ State: _____ Zip: _____

When First Seen: _____
                             Date/Time

When First Captured: _____
                             Date/Time

Where Found: City _____ County _____ State _____

Specific location where animal/bird was found (in yard, etc.): _____

Please circle any information pertaining to the animal/bird:

fell from nest	cat attack	in road	near window	can't stand	nest destroyed
found on ground	hit by car	hit window	limping	cold	wet
bird attack	bleeding	can't fly	panting	staggering	dog attack
shot	in a trap	abused	oiled	exposure to chemicals	
orphaned	easy to catch	hard to catch			

Additional remarks: _____

Did you feed the animal/bird? _____ If yes, what & how? _____

What else did you do to help it? _____

INITIAL MAMMAL EXAM

Common Name: _____ Case #: _____ Date: _____

Presenting Condition: _____

General Appearance: BAR   Lethargic   Dehydrated   Underweight   Unconscious

Weight: _____ Temp: _____ Approx. Age: _____ Sex: Male Female Unknown

Rectal Tone: Yes   No   Parasites: _____ Alopecia: _____

Eyes: Clear   Discharge: _____ Pupil Response: Yes   No

Palpebral Reflex: Yes   No   Comments: _____

Ears: Clean   Discharge: _____ Blood: Yes   No

Comments: _____

Mouth: MM: _____ CRT: _____ seconds   Blood: Yes   No

Teeth: _____ Wounds: _____

Comments: _____

Nose: Clean   Discharge: _____ Blood: Yes   No

Wounds: _____ Comments: _____

Heart: Normal   Heart Rate: _____ Bradycardia   Tachycardia   Murmur _____

Lungs: Clear   Sounds: _____ Breathing: Normal Rapid Shallow Labored

Muscular/Skeletal: Swelling/Lameness: _____ Fractures: _____

                       Reflexes: Good   Poor   None   Circulation: Good Fair Poor

Abdomen: Normal   Distended   Painful   Trauma: _____

Feet: Normal   Wounds: _____ Circulation: Good   Fair   Poor

          Blood: Yes   No   Swelling: Yes   No   Comments: _____

Other Findings: _____ Rehaber's Initials _____

INITIAL AVIAN EXAM

Common Name: _____ Case #: _____ Date: _____

Presenting Condition: _____

General Appearance: BAR   Lethargic   Dehydrated   Underweight   Unconscious

Weight: _____ Temp: _____ Approx. Age: _____ Sex: Male Female Unknown

Rectal Tone: Yes   No   Parasites: _____ Feather Condition: Good Fair Poor

Feather Development: Naked   Down   Pin   ½-Pin   ¼ Pin   Mature   Molt

Posture: Normal   Hock Sitting   Dorsal   Lateral

Head Position: Normal   Abnormal: _____

Skull: Normal   Trauma: _____

Eyes: Clear   Discharge: _____ Color: _____ Comments: _____

Ears: Clear   Discharge: _____ Comments: _____

Mouth: Normal Trauma Color: _____ Choanal Slit: _____ Lesions: _____

                 Crop: Full   Empty   Comments: _____

Nares: Clear   Trauma   Discharge: _____ Sounds: _____

                 Comments: _____

Heart: Normal   Heart Rate: _____

Lungs: Clear   Sounds: _____

Breathing: Normal   Rapid   Shallow   Labored

Abdomen: Normal   Distended   Painful   Trauma: _____

Wings: Normal   Fracture: _____ Dislocation: _____

Legs/Digits: Normal   Fracture: _____ Dislocation: _____

Other Findings: _____ Rehaber's Initials _____

FIRST-AID AVIAN BASICS

Nails

It's easy for nails to get broken, especially when they are too long. You can use styptic powder, silver nitrate sticks, and flour or corn starch to stop the bleeding. First you should wipe off or blot the blood from the nail that is bleeding with a tissue and then apply the product you're using to stop the bleeding.

Blood Feathers

While new feathers are growing in, they have both an artery and vein running through them. A clumsy bird or bird that is thrashing around may break a new feather. These feathers can bleed profusely and can look like they are bleeding even more than they are. The best method for stopping most of these occurrences of blood loss is to have a handy pair of hemostats, fine needle nosed pliers or other instrument to provide you with a good grip and pull the bleeding feather.

This is done by grasping the shaft of the feather above the tear. Hold firmly and pull straight out in the direction the feather is growing. Do not jerk or pull out at an angle as this may cause further tearing. Make sure no skin is in the grip so no skin tearing will occur. Make sure you are familiar with the proper restraint to use. This will decrease chances of injury to yourself and the bird.

Lacerations

The primary goal is to control the bleeding. Apply direct pressure with gauze or other absorbable products available. After the bleeding has stopped do not start cleaning or flushing out the wound. This may wash away the clot and start bleeding again. Wait one hour before attempting to clean the area. This also gives your bird time to rest.

Fractures

The most common fractures in birds are wings and legs. The wing and leg bones of birds are hollow and when they break, are likely to splinter into several pieces. These pieces often have sharp edges that could cause considerable soft tissue damage that may be more problematic than the fracture itself. Your goal is to stabilize the fracture and place the bird in a location that will prevent further injury and keep it calm.

Figure-8 Bandage

Place the injured wing in the normal resting position near the body. Starting inside near the top edge, roll your bandage material around to the top of the wing and diagonal to the opposite edge. Roll around the underside of the wing in a straight line to the opposite underside edge. Then bring the bandage out and roll diagonally upwards and directly opposite of the starting point. You will see an X shape on top of the wing and a == configuration on the underside of the wing. Usually two to three wraps will work, keep in mind not to wrap too tight and the bandage should be stable.

On the last wrap, instead of going upward and diagonally, bring the bandage around the bird's body and under the opposite wing. Remember also that this layer will need to be stable (no slipping) and allow for chest expansion otherwise the bird will not be able to breath. When the bandage is in place, check to ensure the bandaged wing is level with the other wing when folded. This simple check is a quick assurance that the bandaged wing is in proper position.

Wing Splint

With the injured wing, start with your bandage just inside and to the lower part of the wing. Wrap the bandage around the injured wing. Attach the bandage to itself on the original side. Second wrap the upper part of the wing incorporating the body but not the opposite wing. Attach the bandage to itself on the original side. Make sure the bandage is secure; yet loose enough for the bird to breathe. The bird needs to be able to expand its chest in order to breathe. A third strip of bandage material would be placed where the tips of the wings would meet. This bandage goes around the wing tips and tail to offer a counter balance for the splint.

TREATMENT AND RELEASE OF OILED BIRDS

For areas that have been polluted by oil, rescuers must capture affected birds as quickly as possible in order to save them. Minimizing stress is critical for ensuring that captured birds survive.

Once the bird is stable a physical exam should be performed to establish the degree of oiling. Oiled birds may be debilitated either by the toxic effects of ingesting oil, or by exhaustion and starvation. The bird may only have a small patch of oil on it or it may be entirely covered in oil. Initially following the exam, the bird is fed a rehydration solution through a tube inserted orally into the stomach. This helps stabilize the bird so it may regain its strength before the cleaning process. Birds should be discouraged from preening themselves so they do not ingest oil. They should be kept in a warm, quiet environment until they become alert and responsive, and ultimately, ready to be washed. The bird should be allowed to move around, not restrained or prevented from biting by binding its wings, legs, or beak.

The product found to be the most effective at removing oil is Dawn dishwashing liquid. The bird's entire body is immersed in a one percent solution of Dawn and warm water. Keep in mind that once the bird is wet, the bird is unable to thermo regulate, therefore another person should be assisting with the cleansing process in order to finish sooner. A soft toothbrush and cotton swabs are used to loosen dried oil around the head and eye area. When the water becomes dirty, the bird is moved to a second pan. The washing process is repeated as often as necessary and up to 12 tubs are not uncommon to be used. When the tub of water is clear and free of oil, then the bird can be considered clean.

Once cleaned from oil the bird will need to be rinsed thoroughly. Rinsing is just as important as washing because any detergent or solution left on the feathers can impair the natural waterproofing process. Gently rinse and flush the entire area of the bird with a spa propelled type shower head. Do not use a garden hose; you want to avoid damage to the feathers.

Drying the bird should be done with commercial pet grooming dryers, not personal hair dryers. A grate should be placed beneath the bird as to allow air circulation all the way around. Keep the dryer setting on LOW to avoid overheating the bird. Check on the bird every five to fifteen minutes.

An oiled bird is released when it is completely stable, healthy, and when it's waterproofing is determined to be flawless. The bird must exhibit normal feeding, swimming, and diving behavior, and have normal weight for their species. Releases are usually made early in the day, during fair weather, so the bird can adjust to its natural habitat during daylight hours.

VACCINATION PROTOCOLS FOR WILDLIFE

The purpose of in-house vaccination is not to give "herd immunity" but to mitigate effect of disease in unprotected animals in the rehab facility.

Raccoon

Raccoons are susceptible to feline panluekopenia virus (FPV), mink enteritis virus (MEV), and raccoon parvovirus (RPV). Note that raccoons are not susceptible to canine parvovirus (CPV). Canine distemper virus (CDV) known as morbillivirus (related to measles), is highly infectious and contagious. CDV is unstable in the environment but can survive in the affected animal for up to 90 days post infection.

Vaccinate all incoming raccoons with a modified live feline panluekopenia vaccine (e.g. Fel-O-Vac PCT); begin at six weeks of age; continue to vaccinate at four week intervals through 18 weeks of age (if still in your care). In areas near mink ranches, Biovac (used for MEV) can be given on the same schedule to susceptible raccoon orphans. Vaccines should not be given together, separate vaccines by five days. Protocol for CDV protection of juveniles in rehab facility; vaccinate with Fervac-D.

Fox

Distemper is a common disease to canines. Signs of the disease are the same as in dogs with the incubation period being about two weeks. A combined mink vaccine against distemper, botulism, and virus enteritis is sometimes used; however, as virus enteritis does not occur in foxes, and botulism not being a threat in a properly managed facility, it is probably much more appropriate to use a combined canine distemper-hepatitis vaccine. Young animals should receive a first vaccine at eight to ten weeks and a distemper booster vaccination in the winter when about ten months old, if still in your care.

Infectious Canine Hepatitis (Fox Encephalitis) is seen in foxes. Signs of the latter include anorexia, vomiting, diarrhea, jaundice, and convulsion. The virus may be spread by dogs. Prevention is by vaccination (see above distemper). As a single hepatitis vaccination will last for life, the combined vaccine does not need to be used for the booster inoculation.

PREPARING FOR RELEASE

Small Birds

Before releasing small birds they should first be placed in an outdoor enclosure for a couple weeks so they may get acclimated to the environment, sounds, and to their surroundings. They also need to exercise their wings and learn how to navigate before just letting them go, so their outdoor enclosure should be large in size to allow for this. Keep in mind that when you do release these small birds that they need time to get familiar with their new environment and find shelter. Never release small birds early in the morning (before 9:00 a.m.) or late in the evening (after 6:00 p.m.). Predators (hawk, raccoon, fox, and cats) are more prevalent during that time.

Squirrels, Rabbits, Chipmunks, and Other Small Mammals

Before releasing any small mammal they should first be placed in an outdoor enclosure large enough for them to exercise their ability to move quickly and elude predators. They will need a couple weeks to get acclimated to their new environment, sounds, and their surroundings. Feed a diet that they would normally find in the wild and would eat naturally, absolutely no more commercial foods or treats. Once they leave they most likely will never return but maybe for a couple days. Making sure they can find their food sources in their new wild habitat on their own will make it a successful release.

Raccoons

Before releasing raccoons, they should be first prepared for the great outdoors. When they are almost three months old an outdoor enclosure that is large enough for them to demonstrate their climbing abilities should be made. Plenty of logs, branches, rocks, and other things that they would naturally find in the wild should be placed with them. A pool of water should be placed with them with fish (minnows) in the water so they may demonstrate their fishing/water skills. Hiding food under rocks and grass/hay will help them with their ability to search for food. The most thoughtless thing I can imagine is raising an infant raccoon and making it dependent on human care, and then, without prior adjustment, leaving the confused creature in an unfamiliar area. Its first instinct would be to head for the nearest human dwelling. Trusting humans because they are the only parents it knows, the poor little coon is shot, trapped, or hunted by dogs.

Season to Release

Most orphan animals are kept until they are approximately three to four months of age. Being spring or late summer babies this means they may not be released until the fall. Either early or late in the fall, this will most likely be the time you would release birds or mammals back into their natural environment. The only season that is not preferred as a time for release would be the winter for obvious reasons, lack of food, water, and shelter.

SPECIE DISEASES

Opossum

Metabolic Bone Disease

Most often caused by too much protein, or not balancing the diet's calcium/phosphorus ratio. Vitamin A toxicity, often due to offering too many orange and leafy green vegetables or by vitamin supplements, lead to calcium being lost from the system in the urine and may cause renal problems as well. Another cause, offering too much fruit that can cause diuretic symptoms and with it the loss of minerals and calcium.

Signs of Metabolic Bone Disease (MBD)

> Depressed grip in hands/feet and in strength of limbs or tail.
> Depressed activity level
> Loss of appetite, increase water intake
> Delicate stance, appears to "walk on egg shells"
> Extremities seem enlarged
> May see tremors and jerky movements
> Fractures are possible
> Inability to effectively use mouth/jaw parts

Necrotizing Fasciitis/Toxic Shock Syndrome—Flesh Eating Disease

A rapidly moving bacterial disease involving the fascia. The bacteria appears to affect opossums the same way as humans, undermining skin, destroying nerves, vessels, and connective tissue, leading to bruising, severe pain, necrosis of skin and finally the entire bodily system.

Signs of Necrotizing Fasciitis—Skin reddened and bruised, exaggerated pain at site, very hot to the touch.

Signs of Toxic Shock Syndrome—Swelling to the head and neck which may double in size in a couple of hours. Rapid onset of extreme edema, skin reddened and bruised, rapid heart beat, and respiratory distress.

Dermal Septic Necrosis—Crispy Ear Syndrome

Bacteria spread primarily from sites of infection (bites, wounds, broken teeth).

Signs of Dermal Septic Necrosis

> "Crispy Ear" most common, starts out appearing similar as a hematoma in a dog's ear and progresses to the dry form which looks like fly strike or frostbite.
> Craters anywhere on the tail
> May be evidence of bleeding under the nails, decreased circulation to tips and progresses to the entire foot.
> Mouth and nostrils may have crusts
> Abdominal area may have bald patches, scabs, cuts or discoloration.

Raccoon

Canine Distemper Virus

CDV is infectious and highly contagious to raccoons and other animals. It is primarily an aerosol transmission route by contact with oral or ocular fluids. It requires a more direct contact and close association between infected and susceptible raccoons. Canine Distemper Virus is unstable in the environment but can survive in the affected animal for up to 90 days post infection.

Signs of Canine Distemper Virus (CDV)

> Abnormal behavior (out during the daytime)
> Loss of fear
> Aimless wandering
> Incoordination
> Convulsions
> Abnormal "green glow" of eyes.

Parvovirus

Raccoons are susceptible to Feline Panluekopenia virus (FPV), Mink Enteritis Virus (MEV) and Raccoon Parvovirus (RPV).

Note: raccoons are not susceptible to Canine Parvovirus (CPV). Transmission is from fecal to oral route. Extremely high mortality rate, recovered animals shed the virus to others. Any raccoons treated and recovered should not be released back into the wild or it will go on to infect others.

Signs of Parvovirus

> Less than two to three weeks of age will see ataxia.
> Older than four weeks clinical signs vary by degree of damage to intestines but will see malabsorption, loss of tissue fluids and plasma protein, blood resulting in bloody or mucoid diarrhea, lowered white blood cell and neutrophil counts.

Mycoplasma

Manifests as mycoplasma arthritis in raccoons and causes painful swelling, abscess to joints of legs and feet. Infects bone at growth plates, destroys the ability of the bone to elongate as the animal grows. It goes out into soft tissues in and around the joints; swelling is caused from the accumulation of yellow pus in tissues. Antibiotic therapy is not successful and damage to joints and bone are permanent. It is very contagious to others raccoons and is carried in the upper respiratory tract.

Leptospirosis

Caused by bacteria, leptospira comes in many different strains, twelve that I am aware of. It is primarily found in renal tubes and carried through the raccoon's urine. Raccoons are not known for having clinical disease, but act as a host; a zoonotic reservoir for others. It is transmitted via urine and is acquired through contact with mucous membranes, upper respiratory, eyes, and wet or abraded skin. In favorable conditions leptospira can live in water for 16 days and soil for 24 days. Rats are a major vector for human leptospirosis. Use good hygiene, gloves and thorough cleaning.

Red Fox

Sarcoptic Mange

One of the most common diseases and one of the most obvious, that affects foxes is mange caused by the mite Sarcoptes Scabiei. The mite is spread by contact. The mite burrows into the skin and multiplies rapidly causing extensive hair loss and irritation starting at the base of the tail and hind feet and quickly spreading over the rump, back and finally to the head. The fox may lose half its body weight, most of its hair, its eyes and face will become encrusted and eventually the fox will die in about four months.

Sarcoptic mange is contagious to humans and is described as scabies. Anyone handling a fox suspected of suffering from mange should wear an apron and gloves.

Gray and Fox Squirrels

Squirrel Fibroma (pox)

This is a viral disease which produces multiple tumors on the skin of gray and fox squirrels. These tumors are presumably all caused by a virus. Naturally infected squirrels are mostly juveniles. The tumors may be scattered over all the body and range in size from a few mm to 25mm in diameter. Metastasis to the lungs, liver, kidney, and lymph nodes has been reported. In general, there are no obvious signs of illness in naturally infected squirrels except for the presence of the tumors over the skin. In severe cases, when vision is obstructed or the skin becomes secondarily infected, the animal may be less active, weak, and eventually die.

As far as we know, the virus only infects squirrels in nature. However, in the laboratory it has been successfully transmitted to woodchucks and rabbits. Where squirrel fibroma (pox) is common, there apparently have been no noticeable effects on squirrel populations. Current knowledge indicates the virus is not transmissible to humans.

Water Birds

Botulinum Poisoning

During hot or dry weather when water levels fall, mud becomes an ideal breeding ground for the anaerobic bacteria Clostridium botulinum. Water birds, especially gulls, feed from this mud taking in invertebrates and mollusks. The clostridium produces a highly toxic poison that will kill many birds but some will survive long enough to be picked up and taken for treatment.

Signs of Botulinum

>Flaccid paralysis of the legs
>Loss of control of the nictitating membrane
>Shallow irregular heartbeat and depressed breathing
>Could be a non-smelly projectile diarrhea

Dove and Pigeon

Trichomoniasis (Canker)

This is a disease primarily of doves and pigeons and is transmitted from the adult to their offspring by regurgitational method of feeding used by these birds. Other ways of transmitting the disease are by adult birds contaminating food, water, bedding, and during courtship behavior. It is a parasite of the upper digestive tract of many avian species causing accumulation of necrotic material in the mouth and esophagus. It is principally a disease of young birds and is often fatal. Trichomonas gallinae has never been reported to infect humans and is of no public health significance.

Signs of Trichomoniasis

> Depressed, appear listless, ruffled and dull feathers
> Salivate excessively, watery eyes, diarrhea
> Emaciated, difficulty eating and drinking
> Difficulty closing their mouth, display repeated swallowing movements
> Exhibit open mouth and noisy breathing
> Difficulty standing or maintaining balance
> Puffy appearance of the neck
> Exhibit a sunken and empty crop and have an odor
> Necrotic masses (cheese-like) in the mouth are commonly seen

Ornithosis (Chlamydia psittaci)

Ornithosis is caused by the bacterium Chalmydia psittaci responsible for psittacosis in parrots. It is zoonotic so is potentially a dangerous health hazard. The infection has been found in wild pigeons and doves.

Signs of Ornithosis

> Ocular discharge
> Nasal discharge
> Difficult breathing

Paramyxovirus

The virus is mainly transmitted by direct contact from the secretions and excretions of a sick bird. It can also be carried on boots, clothing, boxes, baskets and even in the air as a form of virulent dust. The disease is very contagious although not necessary fatal if the bird can be supported throughout. Only after diarrhea is seen will the nervous systems signs show.

Signs of Paramyxovirus

> Head tremors
> Head tilt upside down
> Lack of coordination
> Paralysis of one wing, then both
> Possibly paralysis of feet

All Birds

Aspergillosis

A result of a fungal infection by one of the Aspergillus species. It thrives in damp, decaying vegetable matter especially moldy or wet hay. Although the fungus needs damp conditions to flourish, its spores are spread though dry conditions like the bottom of a cage. Aspergillus is widespread in the environment. The problem with this disease is that it is hard to detect and by the time clinical signs are observed, the disease is so well advanced that it is impossible to cure.

> The acute form which is fatal within one to seven days shows signs of pneumonia and depression.
>
> The sub-acute form may take up to six weeks to develop and become fatal. Clinical signs may show a respiratory wheeze and open-mouth breathing.
>
> The chronic form takes weeks or months to develop and the signs are similar to those in the sub-acute form with weight loss.

Normally birds that are healthy and kept in a clean environment with good ventilation will not be affected. However, wild birds taken into care are stressed and often sick, making them ideal candidates for infection.

Listed below is not considered a disease but a point of interest when dealing with a sick bird.

Lead Poisoning

This particularly hits swans who take in and digest lead fishing weights and possibly lead shotgun pellets picked up as grit for the gizzard. Geese tend to graze more and so are more at risk of picking up gunshot lead rather than fisherman's weights. If not treated promptly lead poisoning will kill. Legislation was passed banning the smaller sizes of lead fishing weight but there are a large amount left in river banks and on river floors.

Signs of Lead Poisoning

> Anorexia which leads to emaciation
> Lethargy
> Bright green droppings
> Limber neck where the lower part of the neck lies across the bird's back.

COMMONLY USED CONVERSION FACTORS

1000 milligrams (mg) = 1 gram (g) = 1 milliliter (ml) or 1 cubic centimeter (cc)

1000 grams (g) = 1 kilogram (kg)

1000 milliliter (ml) = 1 liter (L)

1 milliliter (ml) = 1 cubic centimeter (cc)

1 pound (lb) = 16 ounces (oz)

1 cup (c) = 8 ounces (oz)

454 grams (g) = 1 pound (lb)

2.2 pounds (lbs) = 1 kilogram (kg)

1 drop = .05 ml or 1/20th ml

5 milliliters (ml) = 1 teaspoon (tsp) = 1/6 fluid ounce (oz)

15 milliliters (ml) = 1 tablespoon (tbsp) = 3 teaspoons (tsp) = ½ fluid ounce (oz)

30 milliliters (ml) = 2 tablespoons (tbsp) = 1 fluid ounce (oz)

65 milligrams (mg) = 1 grain

Abbreviations

SID— Once daily (every 24 hours)

BID— Twice daily (every 12 hours)

TID— Three times daily (every 8 hours)

QID— Four times daily (every 6 hours)

q— One administration "every" (i.e., q 24 hours = every 24 hours)

To convert from degrees Fahrenheit to degrees Celsius
Subtract 32, then multiply by 5 and divide by 9

To convert to degrees Celsius to degrees Fahrenheit
Multiply by 9 and divide by 5, then add 32

PERMIT OVERVIEW

STATE PERMITS

The Department of Natural Resources provides applications and a list of requirements for obtaining a permit to rehabilitate wildlife in your state. This permit is separate from a federal permit and can be more restrictive. Before applying for this permit, it is wise to find out whether your municipality has any restrictions that might affect you possessing any wildlife in your care.

FEDERAL PERMITS

The U.S. Fish & Wildlife Service issues permits under various wildlife laws and treaties at different offices at the national, regional, and/or wildlife port levels.

Permits enable the public to engage in legitimate wildlife-related activities that would otherwise be prohibited by law. Service permit programs ensure that such activities are carried out in a manner that safeguards wildlife. Additionally, some permits promote conservation efforts by authorizing scientific research, generating data, or allowing wildlife management and rehabilitation activities to go forward.

Below is a brief overview of the permits handled by the four permitting programs within the Service. Visit their website to print an application and view the requirements for each of these permits.

Endangered Species regional offices administer native endangered and threatened species permits under the Endangered Species Act. Permits are issued to qualified applicants for the following types of activities: enhancement of survival associated with Safe Harbor Agreements and Candidate Conservation Agreements with Assurances, incidental take associated with Habitat Conservation Plans, recovery, and interstate commerce.

International Affairs is responsible for administering CITES for the United States. They primarily issue permits to import and export species that are protected by CITES and by various other wildlife conservation laws. Some examples of other activities they permit are: take of certain marine mammals; take and interstate and foreign commerce of non-native species protected by the Endangered Species Act, including a captive-bred wildlife registration; cooperative breeding programs for live exotic birds covered by the Wild Bird Conservation Act; and import and transport of injurious wildlife.

Law Enforcement administers permits at regional offices and certain port locations. A permit or license may be issued to qualified applicants for the following activities: to engage in business as a wildlife importer or exporter; import or export wildlife at other than a designated or authorized border or special port, and export and re-export certain CITES wildlife.

Migratory Bird regional offices administer permits for qualified applicants for the following types of activities: falconry, raptor propagation, scientific collecting, rehabilitation, conservation education, migratory game bird propagation, salvage, take of depredating birds, taxidermy, and waterfowl sale and disposal. These offices also administer permit activities involving bald and golden eagles, as authorized by the Bald and Golden Eagle Protection Act.